The Reminiscences of

Vice Admiral Fitzhugh Lee

U. S. Navy (Retired)

U. S. Naval Institute
Annapolis, Maryland
1972

Preface

This manuscript is the result of some taped interviews with Vice Admiral Fitzhugh Lee, U. S. Navy (Retired), in 1970 at his home in Coronado, California. These interviews were conducted by Commander Etta Belle Kitchen, U. S. Navy (Retired) for the Oral History Office in the U. S. Naval Institute.

Admiral Lee has done some minor editing of the transcript. Nevertheless, the reader is asked to bear in mind that he is reading a transcript of the spoken word rather than the written word.

An index is affixed to the text for the greater convenience of the reader.

AUTHORIZATION

The undersigned, Vice Admiral Fitzhugh Lee, U. S. Navy (Retired), does hereby release and assign to the United States Naval Institute all his right, title, restrictions, and interest in two interviews between the undersigned and the Oral History Department of the United States Naval Institute, recorded on 11 July and 9 August 1970 in collaboration with Commander Etta-Belle Kitchen, U. S. Navy (Retired). The tape recordings of the interviews shall be the sole property of the Naval Institute. The copyright in both the oral and transcribed versions of the interviews shall also be the sole property of the Naval Institute.

Signed and sealed this 27th day of APRIL, 1983.

Fitzhugh Lee
Vice Admiral Fitzhugh Lee, U. S. Navy (Retired)

Vice Admiral Fitzhugh Lee, USN, Ret.
At his home, Coronado, California   July 11, 1970
Subject: Biography   by E. B. Kitchen

Miss Kitchen: The Institute is very happy Admiral that you will take the time and effort to do the biography for them because your career is prestigious and we are certain that it will make a valuable addition to the library. I thank you from me and from them on letting us start this biography today.

I note on your biography that you come by your name through a series of prestigious people, starting from our country's earliest days to the Revoluntionary War, and while you were just lucky, maybe you could tell us about your early years and your forebearers.

Admiral Lee: I don't know whether I was lucky or unlucky. I regard this as just an accident of birth. But to set the record straight for you my father was George Mason Lee, who was a career officer in the Army and went to West Point in the class of 1901. His father was General Fitzhugh Lee, who had gone to West Point earlier, and subsequently became a Confederate general in the Civil War at the age of twenty-eight. Later on he was the governor of Virginia for two terms, and was the Consul General of the United States in Havana, Cuba when the MAINE blew up, which gained him a certain amount of notoriety. His father was Sidney Smith Lee, who was a career naval officer, spending his active life in the Confederate and Federal Navies. He was the second Commandant of Midshipmen at the Naval Academy at one time, in 1852, I think. I recall a picture of him hanging in McDonough Hall at Annapolis showing him with a beard almost down to his tummy. He was an older brother of Robert E. Lee, and when Robert E. Lee left the Federal Army to go for Virginia Sidney Smith left with him to join the Confederate Navy. Their father was General Henry Lee, known as Lighthorse Harry Lee, who was a figure in the Revolutionary Army. He had two cousins who were Francis Lightfoot Lee and Richard Henry Lee (brothers), who were signers of the Declaration of Independence and who were prominent in the early political and diplomatic history of the United States.

Miss Kitchen: I wanted to ask you about the influences of your early years. Who were the people who influenced your life in the way it has become?

Admiral Lee: Being an Army "brat," I attended many schools in many places in my youth. One of them was the Bishop Brent School in Baquio in the Philippine Islands, which I attended as a boarder from the ages of about nine through twelve. The head of that school was a man named Remson B. Ogilby, who subsequently became the president of Trinity College in

Hartford, Connecticut. He was one of my early idols, a wonderful man who probably inspired me as much as any one else in my life. The school is still there in the Philippines - it's now called the Baquio Boy's School, or the Brent School. It was the only English speaking school for young boys in the Orient in those years, so we had a multinational group of the sons of American and European fathers from Borneo, Java, Japan, and China.

The Naval Academy was the twentieth school that I attended, so when I speak of Dr. Ogilby as being an influence, he was one of a great many other teachers, very few of whom I can recall at the present time.

Miss Kitchen: What about the person in your family that influenced you the most?

Admiral Lee: Well, my mother and father always had a happy home; we had no major problems. I had one sister, and my mother and father probably influenced me as much as anybody else. I had no quarrels with them, admired them both, and they influenced me for the good.

Miss Kitchen: You were born where?

Admiral Lee: I was born in a place called Camp McGrath, which is near the town of Batangas, one hundred miles south of the city of Manila in the Philippine Islands in August of 1905. My father was then stationed in the Philippines as a young lieutenant in the Army.

Miss Kitchen: Did you not go to school in France at one time?

Admiral Lee: My father was a member of the Army of Occupation in Europe after World War I. We lived in Coblenz, Germany, and later he was transferred to what was known as the Graves Registration Service in Paris, which had the job of collecting the remains of all the U. S. Army and other federal people who were lost in World War I and arranging for their burial or for their shipment home. For a year in Paris I attended a French public high school called the Lycée Janson-de-Sailly.

Miss Kitchen: Were you influenced by your stay in France of which you have any recollection?

Admiral Lee: Well, it made me learn French, which was helpful, and always has been. It was also interesting because my mother was much interested in art and music. We traveled a lot and we went to all the operas in Paris. Actually we lived in a boarding house just outside of Paris in a town called Sevres which was a training school for opera run by an ex-French opera star. This man had been impressed with the plight of the great numbers of French soldiers who were blinded by poison gas in World War I and conceived the idea that if they had a singing voice they could serve usefully as singers in the choruses of operas. So he sought out these young blinded soldiers and trained them as singers in his boarding school for singing. As a part time job in those years, I used to take about six or eight of these young blind men on a trolley car and a subway into Paris. This occurred at least once and sometimes twice a week. We sat in a box at the opera which the school permanently rented. They listened to the opera and I had to explain to them what was going on on the stage so that they could understand the action better, and then bring them home. It made quite an impression on me because I was brought home to the troubles that beset young soldiers, their ideas on life, whether or not they felt bitter, and things like that. None of them did. I was fifteen at the time. Most of them were about twenty or twenty-one.

Miss Kitchen: Also, you learned a lot of opera which would not have been in your background otherwise, I'd suspect.

Admiral Lee: Yes, but it didn't last very well.

1 Lee - 6

Miss Kitchen: I note that you were appointed to the Academy by President Harding in 1922, and because of the Army background, I'm interested in why you went to the Academy, and in fact that you were appointed by President Harding.

Admiral Lee: This is a story I've often had to tell -- why I went to the Naval Academy when my father was from a long line of Army people. The true story is as follows: my father, being a career Army officer, had not been able to establish a state residence, even in Virginia, where I could be appointed to West Point. He came home one day and said that he was sorry that he couldn't find any appointment for West Point for me and that I would have to take my choice of working my way through college or going to the Naval Academy. At the Naval Academy they had some vacancies on the presidential list, which was usually reserved for the sons of Army and Navy officers, so I was appointed by President Harding, who was president at the time, and I was able to qualify. I was the fifteenth on a list of fifteen that got in.

Miss Kitchen: Did you feel bad about going to the Academy?

Admiral Lee: No, I liked it. My first cousin, whom I'd known well as a contemporary and pal, had gone to the Naval Academy two years before. I was quite thrilled with the idea of going there and getting out of the Army.

1 Lee - 7

Miss Kitchen: And, of course, some of your ancestors from some years back had been certainly prominent in the Academy.

Admiral Lee: Yes, one did: Sidney Smith Lee.

Miss Kitchen: Can you tell me about some of your experiences while you were at the Academy?

Admiral Lee: I was just another midshipman. I was interested in writing and I had some talent in drawing. I spent a lot of time drawing and writing for the Naval Academy publications -- the Log, which was the magazine; the Lucky Bag, which was the annual; and for the Trident, which was the literary magazine. I helped to illustrate the Naval Academy Song Book, which is still being published.

Miss Kitchen: Were you interested in athletics?

Admiral Lee: I had to be interested. All midshipmen had to be in those days. I went out for swimming and crew for all of my four years. We had spring practice for crew and fall practice for crew, and in the winter we swam. I wasn't very good at either.

Miss Kitchen: Did you have any trouble with the academic work?

Admiral Lee: No, I was fairly well grounded in the things that were needed, and got by.

Miss Kitchen: Your French helped you, too.

Admiral Lee: Yes, I stood one in French in my class. A Filipino, of a Spanish family, stood one in Spanish. They were the only two languages taught in those years.

Miss Kitchen: Do you remember any incidents or anecdotes between you and your classmates that should be included in your biography?

Admiral Lee: I can't think of any that come to my mind other than the fact that your associations throughout the rest of your Navy life, if you stay in it for some forty years as I did, seem to be concentrated, usually, in the people who were at the Naval Academy with you. You remember them well - your own class, the class before you, and the class that followed you as you went through the Academy.

Miss Kitchen: And you served with them time and time again.

Admiral Lee: You served with them and you knew them well, and you corresponded with them through the years as they got into positions of responsibility in the Navy. It certainly has a tremendous influence on the Navy — the fact that in those years almost all of the graduates of the Naval Academy furnished almost all of the officers of the Navy.

Miss Kitchen: And all of the leadership when we got into a war.

Admiral Lee: If we hadn't had that core of professional people who had the same indoctrination — with both its good and bad connotations, most of which were very good — if we hadn't had that training and indoctrination and education together, I think that our success in periods of great expansions as in World War I and World War II would have been much less effective than they were.

Miss Kitchen: Was it not helpful when you saw an order or an operation, whatever, if you knew the man who did it? Was it not helpful to evaluate not only what happened but what caused it to happen?

Admiral Lee: I suppose so. I never thought of it at the time. You knew that he thought in the same thought channels that you did, as a general rule, and recognized it instinctively without thinking about it.

Miss Kitchen: What we're saying is because of this common background you had easier communication.

Admiral Lee: This is true. We spoke the same language.

Miss Kitchen: Right. And you have the same background and training. So you graduated on June 3rd, 1926. How did you happen to stay at the Academy for just a short time?

Admiral Lee: That was the first summer that the U. S. Navy tried to do something about indoctrinating young officers in aviation. They started a summer program at the Naval Academy for young officers staying for three months after graduation. They were given aviation indoctrination in some big flying boats (F5-L's) that were brought to the Naval Academy for that purpose and flew from buoys in the Severn River.

Miss Kitchen: Did you like it?

Admiral Lee: I enjoyed it, yes.

Miss Kitchen: Did you have an opportunity to go into aviation then?

Admiral Lee: No. We were required to serve for two years as a line officer after we graduated before we could enter aviation, and I did so serve.

Miss Kitchen: You went aboard what ship?

Admiral Lee: I was originally sent to the battleship, OKLAHOMA, one of the last Navy ships with reciprocating engines as the main power plant.

In the second part of my two year stint in the line Navy I put the U.S.S. LEXINGTON, the first LEXINGTON, into commission as one of the junior fire control officers. It was commissioned in Boston at the Fall River plant of the Bethlehem Shipbuilding Corporation. There was a commissioning ceremony, and on that occasion the sponsors of the ship traditionally give a gift of silver to the ship concerned. The LEXINGTON was named after the Battle of Lexington, but the city of Lexington, Kentucky, saying that it had several thousand people, wanted to participate in giving the silver service. The town of Lexington, however, which had something like eight hundred people in it at the time said no, we will give the silver service. The ceremony, at about ten degrees below zero, as I recall, was held on the hangar deck of the LEXINGTON. The silver service, which was to be unveiled at the ceremony, was on a mess table and was covered with a green baize cloth. The Mayor of Lexington read his talk presenting the silver service to the ship. During his talk everyone was very embarrassed because the small size of the bumps under the cloth indicated that Lexington, Massachusetts hadn't been able to afford very much in the way of a silver service. But he unveiled it and said that it was all they could give. It was a sugar bowl and creamer of silver made by Paul Revere. It was a good gesture. I've never known what became of it.

Miss Kitchen: It was priceless, of course. It would be a museum piece. I hope it was not lost when the LEXINGTON went down.

Admiral Lee: No, I'm sure it wasn't on the ship when it went down.

Miss Kitchen: You were on the LEXINGTON for a year?

Admiral Lee: Yes, a year on the LEXINGTON and a year on the OKLAHOMA.

Miss Kitchen: Do you have any anecdotes about your assignments or your shipmates?

Admiral Lee: Not particularly in those years. I was very imbued with aviation by the presence on board of the fighter squadrons of the LEXINGTON, and got to know some of the pilots. I couldn't wait until I could get to Pensacola and be one of them.

Miss Kitchen: How soon did you apply?

Admiral Lee: I went as soon as I could, which was in June of 1928.

Miss Kitchen: I have a note which says the LEXINGTON made a speed run to Hawaii in the fastest time that —

Admiral Lee: Yes, this is true. We went from San Pedro to Hawaii at a speed of around thirty knots, as I recall. The phrase which always stuck in our minds, and which I still hear, is that "nothing so big ever went so far, so fast."

Miss Kitchen: Were you impressed with it at the time?

Admiral Lee: Well, when it went that fast it vibrated to beat the band and we had some four days and nights of steady vibration, which was hard on the fillings of your teeth, but otherwise uneventful.

Miss Kitchen: Did they give you quite a welcome in the Islands?

Admiral Lee: I can't recall one, if they did. I probably had the watch.

Miss Kitchen: So then you went to flight training?

Admiral Lee: Yes. Incidentally, while I was attached to the OKLAHOMA, young officers were given a screening test for flight training. I was in San Diego Harbor at that time, and I was allowed to take flight instruction under Navy flight instructors in a little stick and wire type plane - no brakes, no way for the instructor to talk to the student in flight. I made my first solo hop from what is now called Brown Field, an airport on Otay Mesa, near San Diego. The area around there is densely populated now. At that time it was an oat field and my solo hop was made in oats that were up over the top of the wheels.

Miss Kitchen: Do you have any recollection of who your flight instructor was for that experience?

Admiral Lee: His name was Dyer, a pleasant man.

Miss Kitchen: Can you tell me some of your experiences in Pensacola?

Admiral Lee: They were the routine of the people that go through flight training, I imagine. One minor incident which I recall - we were given catapult training on little single float seaplanes that sat on an air compressed catapult, which made for a fast, sharp ride. These planes were not really fitted for catapulting in the way of comfort for the pilot and they had nothing for your head to go back against except a board from an orange crate which was stuck in back of your neck just before you were shot off. When my head hit it the board broke and the jagged pieces of wood cut the back of my neck and caused a good deal of bleeding. I thought this was the end of my life because I had been catapulted off with a lot of velocity and this sudden pain - I didn't know what had happened - and I saw blood all over me. But it really wasn't much. I just landed routinely. I was still bleeding a lot, and I wasn't sure that I would ever want to continue in that type of aviation.

Another incident was when we were given training in ship gunfire spotting, in which we worked with signal books. We were supposed to send signals on the radio to indicate how the shells were landing. I was busy with my signal book, which was a registered publication, and the pilot made a sudden maneuver which resulted in the signal book going over the side. It had a lead plate in its back to make it sink in case of going into the water so the code wouldn't be compromised. It went into a swamp. I thus became the custodian of a registered publication which had been lost. They made me hunt in that swamp for two days to try and find this publication to make sure that it hadn't fallen into unfriendly hands. I thought that was a stupid thing to do.

Miss Kitchen: I take it you didn't find it?

1 Lee - 16

Admiral Lee: No, I didn't find it. It took me about another three weeks of paper work to get exonerated from the crime.

Miss Kitchen: You didn't ever have a letter of anything in your record, I hope.

Admiral Lee: No, this was what the three weeks was about – to determine whether I should have a letter in my record or not.

Miss Kitchen: Who were some of the people with whom you went through flight training?

Admiral Lee: We were assigned in threes in primary formation flight training. One of the two students who happened to be assigned to train with me was a bugler. They were hunting for enlisted men with pilot aptitute at that time, and he had a rating of bugler and subsequently became an officer, and a very good one. The other one was then Captain Halsey, who was one of the senior officers brought back for indoctrination training as a pilot and then given their wings. This was not to make pilots out of them, but to give them some flight indoctrination to better fit them for aviation commands. This was a pretty rugged experience for me. Although I admired and liked Admiral Halsey a lot, he was awfully difficult to fly in formation with.

What the problem was I never really knew until I read his biography in subsequent years. It told of his troubles in flight training, and one of them was he was afraid to wear his glasses because he thought he wouldn't qualify for aviation if he did. Consequently he couldn't read any of the numbers on the instrument panel of the airplane. He didn't know how fast he was going nor where he was going, nor his altitude.

Miss Kitchen: That would be a handicap.

Admiral Lee: It seemed to me it was at the time.

Miss Kitchen: At one time when you were in Pensacola, was he not the commanding officer?

Admiral Lee: You're speaking of a later time when I went back to Pensacola as a flight instructor. Then he was the Chief of Naval Air Training.

Miss Kitchen: Do you have any other items you want to describe of that period?

Admiral Lee: No. It was routine life of people going through flight training in those years. We had an awful lot of fun and loved it.

Recently I saw an old photograph of my flight class when we graduated. Something like eight out of the thirteen became admirals or generals in later life. Among them was Paul Stroop, Donald Felt, David Shoup of the Marines who busted out of flight training at the end, and Admiral Deurfeldt.

Miss Kitchen: Then what was your next duty?

Admiral Lee: I was assigned to Fighting Squadron Five at the Naval Air Station in North Island - this was the squadron known as the Red Rippers. It was a name they had given themselves and they wore fancy red scarves. Other squadrons had other colors. This was the era of leather puttees and riding breeches and leather helmets and goggles, and scarves flying in the wind.

Miss Kitchen: You were based aboard the LEXINGTON at that time?

Admiral Lee: Yes. I went back to the carrier, LEXINGTON, for two years. The Red Rippers participated, while on the LEXINGTON and sometimes on her sister ship the SARATOGA, in the making of HELLS ANGELS, one of the earlier aviation movies.

Miss Kitchen: Did you help in that movie?

Admiral Lee: I was in that movie at various times, mostly as nothing but the pilot of an airplane seen from a distance. The whole company went down to Panama with us and took a lot of scenes on the way.

Those were the years of the first struggles of carrier aviation and the U. S. Navy in demonstrating the effectiveness of carrier air power as part of our national strength. We did this in two big fleet maneuvers. I remember one going out and attacking Pearl Harbor to show how it could be attacked by air, and also another one going down to Panama and attacking the Panama Canal. In both of these fleet problems it was pretty well shown that the defenses of those places were not equal to the potential of the carrier forces in destroying them.

Miss Kitchen: Were you interested at that time in enhancing air power?

Admiral Lee: Yes, I think we all were. As young officers, we were thinking more of the thrills of day to day flying but we were also exposed to the early struggles between the Army Air Corps and carrier aviation - their fusses as to who could contribute most, and whether or not we could have one air force. As one of the younger ones involved, I became dedicated to the point of view of the Navy and rather fanatic about it to some degree, but we were convinced that we had something which nobody had ever had before and which would be useful to the country. We wanted to do everything we could to guard it, nurture it, make it grow, make it be appreciated.

Miss Kitchen: I am interested in the fact that you were always aware of a conflict between Army Air and Navy Air, and you have some material that I think would be of interest.

Admiral Lee: My father and General Billy Mitchell were good friends. They were classmates at West Point, I believe. Anyway, they knew each other well. Our families knew each other well when I was growing up. One of my earlier recollections was a visit to my father, who was then the commanding officer of a horse breeding station for the U. S. Calvary in Front Royal, Virginia. I was then a junior officer in the Navy and was just leaving to go down to Pensacola for flight training and the Mitchells came to visit us. General Mitchell, then Colonel Mitchell, said he was awfully sorry I had decided to go in the Navy. He thought it was a wasted effort but that if I did go in, at least he was glad that I had the good sense to go into aviation which was the only thing that could be worth anything in the future. He was a Douhet man from the start to the finish. Douhet is the name of an Italian general who formulated the doctrine that air power would be omnipotent in all conflicts between nations. It's a theory well known to all military historians. It holds that a massive bomber attack will wipe out the other country before anything can be done about it, so the way to win a war quickly is to bomb it into extinction or submission in the first two days and then you've got it. Modifications of this view still prevail in some quarters.

Miss Kitchen: If we didn't have to have guided missiles.

Admiral Lee: There's lots of ramifications to it that have occurred through the years, and I've been interested in following them. This was a thing which we were thinking about in our earlier struggles in naval aviation and our subsequent troubles in Washington as to the roles and missions of the armed forces, which rightly or wrongly, fortunately or unfortunately, have lasted over a great many years and have resulted in many personality conflicts and philosophical conflicts in the armed forces. They have never been entirely resolved and continue to some extent today. Conflict and competition (which usually is a source material for conflict) are good. Many good things have resulted for the security of our nation because we did have these differences of opinion and these conflicts through the years in trying to figure out how best the armed forces should be organized and what part aviation should play in them.

When I left Fighting Squadron Five, I was ordered to duty as a flight instructor in Pensacola, which pleased me a great deal. But before I got there an article by me was published called, "Some Thoughts on Carrier Design," which was rather presumptious of me as a j.g. who didn't know anything about it. It did create something of a stir and it was concluded that my article couldn't be published in the Naval Institute because of security considerations, but it would be published in the Office of Naval Intelligence Bulletin, which was a confidential publication. It was, and attracted the eye of some higher-ups in Washington and as a result, Captain A. B. Cook had me transferred, much against my own wishes, to be a member of the War Plans Division of OPNAV. I then became for two years the junior officer on duty in the Navy Department. This, I found, involved several extraneous duties - one being that I was an honorary pallbearer at every Arlington funeral for an admiral who didn't have enough contemporaries in the area to serve as pallbearers. I was volunteered for that service, of course. The other one was that because I was a bachelor I was assigned to be one of the potted palms at the White House. These are called aides to the President, but that's what they are -- potted palms at the White House.

Miss Kitchen: The President at that time was President Roosevelt. Did you ever meet him?

Admiral Lee: Oh yes, many times. When I first arrived, President Hoover was in the White House and I served with the Hoovers for about six months or a year, and then the election came, and I served the rest of my time, which was about another year, year and a half, with the Roosevelts. The contrast was quite interesting.

Miss Kitchen: Tell me about that.

Admiral Lee: Their personalities were very different.

I think there were about twenty of us White House aides. We were usually escorts to be on call for ceremonies, or help serve at small dinners, and be a guest when they needed an extra man, and things like that.

Miss Kitchen: You don't mean really to serve?

Admiral Lee: Not at the table, to serve as a social aide. In those years the White House used to have what were called small dinners, about eighteen or twenty people as a rule. One aide was given the duty of being at the White House that evening and receiving the guests invited for dinner and introducing them all to each other, none of whom the aide had ever known before and most of whom didn't know each other. Then when you got them all introduced, you went up and got the President and his Lady and escorted them down. Then you had to introduce all the guests to the President and his Lady.

This was the year I took my memory course - The Roth Memory Course - by mail. In my first weeks I found that I busted on my introductions so much that I determined that I was going to do better - so I took the course, and it helped.

You often went out with the First Lady when she planted trees and did that kind of thing, dedications of buildings, visits to orphanges. If she felt that it was useful, she would ask to have a military aide go along with her to handle the shovel or whatever it was that had to be done in planting a tree.

Miss Kitchen: Do you have any episodes of either the Hoovers or the Roosevelts?

Admiral Lee: Many, but they are all personal in nature.

I can remember the tremendous long lines of the White House receptions, and an aide always having to make the introductions. Poor President Hoover loathed them because his hands would swell up and get hot and feverish from shaking too many hands. So at Hoover receptions, I remember vividly that he always stood in front of a little three-fold screen. Behind the screen was a big bowl of ice and water. The reception would be stopped from time to time while Mr. Hoover went back and soaked his hand in ice water so he could keep on receiving. I thought that was an extraordinary thing for a national leader to have to do in the discharge of his duties.

The Roosevelts just loved receptions and the Hoovers, I think, just loathed them.

Miss Kitchen: Complete difference in personalities. Do you have any stories of Mr. Roosevelt or Mr. Hoover?

Admiral Lee: I was among the taller of the aides, and President Roosevelt was tall, and so I had the job quite a good deal - shared it with only one or two others - of being his crutch because he couldn't walk really without crutches. He would grab my arm very strongly with his very strong fist. You almost had to carry him, but he managed to walk. He always liked in public appearances to be shown walking, so I spent considerable time as a strong right arm, so to speak. He used a cane on one side and grabbed your arm on the other side and that way he was able to do a very slow, shuffling walk. But he liked to do that rather than show himself to be really a wheel chair man, which he was.

Miss Kitchen: It must have taken a lot of guts.

Admiral Lee: It did. You had a great deal of admiration for him in every aspect of overcoming his physical handicaps. As his crutch I was close to Mr. Roosevelt on many occasions and listened to him talk and joke, and had a lot of conversations with him that were interesting but nothing of any great significance.

I was much concerned about Mr. Howe, who was in the White House at that time, and whom I thought then, although I couldn't say why, wasn't a very good influence; also Mr. Harry Hopkins, whom the aides didn't like very much. I really don't know why. We just felt they were sort of political string pullers, and were telling Roosevelt what to do sometimes when maybe someone else should have been there telling him to do something else.

Miss Kitchen: Did you think their advice was not for the welfare of the country?

Admiral Lee: I certainly didn't think so at the time, very far from it. But in my readings in history since, I think there was some reason for that being true.

Miss Kitchen: Did you ever sit in on any conferences with Mr. Roosevelt and any of his aides?

Admiral Lee: No, from the point of business conferences, getting things done of an official or political nature, no.

Miss Kitchen: Do you have any episodes of Mrs. Roosevelt?

Admiral Lee: Well, she was a very dominating woman, very strong willed, and who got her way. She was always gracious in public to everybody, extremely so, and you felt that she was a remarkable woman. When she wanted something done, and an aide had to help and it wasn't done well, she could let go and let him have it pretty strongly. This made an impression on me — that she had a job to do; that she was trying to do it the very best she could and she would not fail to assert whatever authority she needed in order to get anything done that she wanted done. And I think she did that all her life.

Miss Kitchen: Do you feel that she influenced the President?

Admiral Lee: Yes. I think every wife influences her husband.
Practically all of my associations with the Roosevelts and the Hoovers were social — public social affairs. It was interesting and you met a great many prominent people because they were invited to the White House. At these small dinners that I mentioned, the aide's job was always to show them all into the dining room. With Mrs. Hoover, you were then allowed to go off on your own, but with Mrs. Roosevelt you had to have a "blue plate special" alone in another small dining room and and then you had to be available for being socially nice after dinner.

Miss Kitchen: But she didn't invite you to sit down with the guests?

Admiral Lee: Sometimes we were asked but usually only when they needed an extra man. Sometimes you went, not counting on having to stay for dinner, and found out you had to stay.

Miss Kitchen: So you were on call all the time?

Admiral Lee: We were on a regular watch list. You had the duty and when anything was wanted you were called. I think the same process is still going on.

Miss Kitchen: You spoke of being ordered to the War Plans Division because of the article you wrote, and I wonder if you were able to pursue that or if your ideas were adopted when you were on this new assignment?

Admiral Lee: No, the actual matter of carrier design never came into the picture at all for me when I was there. I found out that the reason I had been ordered up there was that there was no aviator on duty in War Plans Division, and Captain Cook, who was then in the Bureau of Aeronautics, felt that there shoul be. They said that they could use some aviation thinking around the office, I suppose, and he felt that maybe I, having had some thoughts about carrier warfare, could be useful - and there I was.

Actually I spent most of my time in two ways. One was as an assistant to a captain, I think his name was Griswold, and we worked for eight hours a day meticulously drawing up the numbered and colored war plans. I was then working as a sort of bookkeeper, so to speak, in the formulation of what became the Orange and Rainbow plans - the war plans which were put into effect when war came at Pearl Harbor. This usually involved mechanical computations, figuring how you would expand industry and how many planes you would have to build, how many factories you would have to get to build them.

Captain Griswold was a very meticulous, dedicated man who worked with five pencils that all had to be very sharp, and had a tiny handwriting which was hard to read. I was his assistant and fact getter and pencil sharpener.

The other part of this was ---

Miss Kitchen: That must have taught you a great deal, though.

Admiral Lee: Yes and no. It was all very nebulous. But it got me very much interested in the Pacific Islands, which were all then under the control of Japan - the Trust Territory - and we were doing a great deal in trying to learn more about them - something Japan didn't want us to do. This came back into my life much later on. I was interested in plans on how to get seaplanes for the western Pacific in those years.

The other aspect of my job was really interesting, and had influences later in my career. This stemmed from the fact that I was listed in the Directory of the Office of Naval Intelligence. I was given an additional billet as the aviator in O.N.I. because they didn't have any aviators there either. I appeared in the Directory as the Aviation Representative of the Office of ONI. This immediately got me into the clutches of the foreign naval attaches in Washington, who figured I was their contact for all aviation matters. I was persistently and pleasantly entertained by lots of them for this reason, but particularly by the Japanese. They had about eight young language officers in their Washington embassy, who thought that one access to information was through being extremely nice to and entertaining the ONI Aviation Representative. They had one special asset in this business because these were were the years of prohibition in the United States and the embassies had diplomatic immunity from prohibition. I was plied with gifts of Johnny Walker Black Label Whiskey all the time, I couldn't accept these as formal gifts. But I could go to their houses and when they came to the bachelor apartment that I shared with Captain (then Lieutenant) Ford N. Taylor, they would usually come with a bottle or two of Black Label Whiskey to add pleasure to the evening. I suppose this helped out in the exchange of intelligence. It did lead to many contacts with the Japanese which paid off in some respects after I went out to the China Station later on and visited in Japan.

Miss Kitchen: Can you amplify that?

Admiral Lee: Yes. When I left Washington, I was ordered to the Asiatic Fleet. I also became the number two aviator in seniority in the Asiatic Fleet - there were a very small number out there. At that time we were having a fuss with the Japanese about the exchange of military intelligence on a give and take basis. We were complaining that nobody in our embassy in Tokyo was allowed to see anything and we were letting their military and naval attaches wander all over the United States and see everything. So it was decided that I would be sent up to Japan as a temporary member of the American embassy staff. I would be shown all about naval aviation that the Japanese wanted to show me. A young Army Air Corps man accompanied me, representing Army Aviation. The two of us were shown all over Japan for three month tours in three successive years. The Japanese were to show us all the things that they wanted to; this was to be the basis of what their attaches would be shown in the United States so it would be on a more quid pro quo basis.

I met again in Japan several of the men who had been language students in Washington, and they did show me around in Japan, and were nice to me. It was an interesting experience - out of this world in many respects because we traveled all over in the parts of Japan that foreigners very rarely went to. The gist of it was, however, that we were drowned in tea drinking and saki drinking wherever we went, but were shown practically nothing. We never saw one Japanese carrier. We would go to a naval station and the station would be cleaned out of all the aircraft squadrons based there, and the ships that were based there would all be taken out. We would be shown the naked air station. Just for one little j.g. - it seemed almost silly. I would write home that I had gotten to see almost nothing. I was shown all their installations, and shown charts and pictures, and questions asked were sometimes answered, but I would see nothing of any of their combat airplanes or their combat ships. They never did show me one the whole time. But there was a great deal of socializing and traveling around in Japan which was interesting.

Miss Kitchen: Did our nation follow through and restirct the Japanese?

Admiral Lee: Yes, and as a result of this, I believe - I left China in '36, which was five years before Pearl Harbor - there ensued more of an open exchange.

Commander Ralph Oftsie, a naval aviator, was assigned to the embassy in a permanent job, taking my itinerant place, and as a result of his efforts and others, we later had a greater exchange of information. But it was always on a very stalking, pussycat type of approach to each other - trying to see how much you could conceal and how much you could let go and learn from the other fellow what you thought you needed and which he wouldn't think would be valuable to you, and that sort of thing.

1 Lee - 33

We didn't learn much except that we did become quite well convinced, I'm sure, that we were very superior to them in naval aviation. I think that the war years showed that we were basically ahead of them a good deal.

Miss Kitchen: Were you aware that they were preparing for a war?

Admiral Lee: Oh yes, very definitely.

Miss Kitchen: Tell me about that.

Admiral Lee: Let's turn to today. Why is Russia building up a great navy and now has a fleet bigger than the Sixth Fleet in the Mediterranean, which has been our forward puddle of influence of the last two decades?

You're aware because of the things you know they build and how they were training for it and also by what they say.

Miss Kitchen: But you didn't see anything. How many places were you able to see?

Admiral Lee: Well, I think in the course of my visit to Japan I was taken to every major naval installation having anything to do with naval aviation in Japan of any significance whatsoever, and lots of army aviation stations as well.

Miss Kitchen: How many would that have been?

Admiral Lee: Twenty-five, thirty — seeing a lot of them more than once. You could see their docks; you could see their big hangars; you could see all the offices and their research things with all the research planes taken away before you went there.

I was taken to a research center at Oppama, near Yokohama, and went into a hangar where a big canvas curtain screened half of it from my view. There were often things like that — great big canvas covers draped around things I was not allowed to look at. By hapenstance, at Oppama, as we were walking around, somebody had left the whole side of this canvas curtain open and I looked in and saw a big flying boat made by the Martin people to sell to the U. S. Navy. The Navy hadn't bought it but the Martin people had sold it to Japan. Our government knew about it and was willing that it be done. I said, "What are you concealing this thing from me for? I saw that same airplane back in Washington years ago." They laughed about it and took me in and let me look around at it and we compared notes about it — about how they built their boats and so forth. It didn't discomfort them much that I had sort of caught them this way. They laughed about it but it was indicative of this sort of silly approach to the whole problem.

I should add that I did see a lot of the little planes used for primary flight training. It was the combat aircraft which were concealed from me.

1 Lee — 35

Miss Kitchen: Was there comaraderie between you as an aviator and them as aviators that wouldn't have been otherwise?

Admiral Lee: Yes, they were aviation people I was going with. Three or four of the young Japanese language students I knew in Washington were naval aviators. They subsequently became pretty high ranking officers in the Japanese navy fighting against us.

Miss Kitchen: Do you remember any of their names?

Admiral Lee: Yes, Ahiro Sasaki was one of my best friends. I saw him in subsequent years in the 1950's in Japan and he was a little retired farmer on a little tiny plot of land outside of Iwakuni — agricultural Japan — penniless, as were all of the officers who had been prominent in the war. After the war they were retired without pay and had to take any menial job they could find. Sasaki was the air officer on the AKAGI, one of the big Jap carriers at Midway.

Miss Kitchen: I'm interested in that period in Asia. What was your basic assignment out there in the Pacific?

Admiral Lee: There were two naval aviation units in the Asiatic Fleet. One was called the Aircraft Utility Unit of the Asiatic Fleet: this consisted of two big old Martin twin float seaplanes which were based on an ex-mine sweeper called the HERON, scarcely more than an overgrown tugboat. It had a wide fantail on which you could hoist, with a crane, one plane at a time. So for eighteen months we flew around the western Pacific based on the HERON. We moored the planes to buoys near the ship and hoisted one of them on the ship occassionally for upkeep. For the long trips to northern China or elsewhere these two big seaplanes were placed on a oil tanker. (Incidentally, the tanker for most of my trips out there was the old PECOS which was subsequently sunk in the Java Sea in dramatic circumstances in the war.) I was the Officer in Charge of the utility unit based on the HERON, which was commanded by a lieutenant, but he was on the sick list for a lot of time out there and I was the acting commanding officer and actual executive officer as well, also Officer-In-Charge of the Utility Unit.

Our principal duty was to furnish target services for all ships of the Asiatic Fleet. We towed big target sleeves for them to shoot at with anti-aircraft guns. We chased the torpedoes of the destroyers and the cruisers. When they fired torpedoes in excess, we would chase the torpedoes and mark them at the end of their run with flags and buoys, so they could subsequently be found.

We had many other miscellaneous messenger and ambulance duties and things of that sort, and utility things, mapping services, things that were very interesting. But our basic duty was to assist gunnery training exercises.

I was then transferred to the AUGUSTA which was commanded by Captain Chester Nimitz at that time. I was the second senior of the aviators on board for the four single-float little seaplanes the AUGUSTA carried. These were carried on the ship at all times. They were the spotting planes for the ship - a part of her military armament. We used to serve as sort of advanced navigators in some places when the ship went into unchartered waters. There is an awful lot of unchartered coral in the South China Sea, around Singapore and such places. We would fly ahead of the ship, talking by radio to the navigator saying, "You're heading for a reef. Slow up, stop, back," or something like that, which he had to do in going into places such as near the Pratas Reef, and in the China Sea, and into ports such as Jesselton in North Borneo and Balikpapan and Pontianak in Dutch Borneo, where the ships went sometimes to pay the crew because you got a better exchange rate in a Dutch port. I had three years of that all over the China Station, and it was all fascinating to me.

Miss Kitchen: I think we ought to go back and describe how you got from your last duty in Washington out to your duty in the Asiatic Fleet.

Admiral Lee: I am an impulsive and avid sightseer and traveler and I got something like three months leave between stations, plus travel time, which is unheard of today but which could be accumulated in those years. I had never taken any leave in Washington.

I was ordered to the AUGUSTA, which was slated to be the flag ship of the Asiatic Fleet. The AUGUSTA was in Seattle and sailing for Shanghai. I was allowed to go on my own from Washington to join the AUGUSTA when she got to China. I did this by getting on an American freighter in Norfolk and sailing as the only passenger on the ship to Rotterdam.

There I got off and sort of hitch-hiked my way down to Constantinople (now Istanbul) through northern France, Holland, Belgium, Germany, Czechoslovakia, Austria, Hungary, Yugoslavia, Bulgaria, and Anatolian Turkey to Constantinople. From there I took a little Italian tourist steamer through the Greek Islands, to the island of Rhodes and Haifa and Jaffa in Palestine. I went also to Beirut and other ports along the Levantine coast, and ended up in Suez where I got off and went and rode a camel through the pyramids and saw Cairo. Then I got a small Japanese freighter at Suez, which took me to Colombo through the Red Sea.

The hottest time I ever spent in my life was going down wind through the Red Sea in a Japanese coal burning freighter. The firemen in the fire room could only shovel coal for twenty minutes; then they had to go topside and doused with salt water hoses. Then they would go back to stoking the boilers for another twenty minutes. That's the way they went through the Red Sea because it was so hot, and it's a long trip - about as far as from New York to Miami, about a four day voyage.

In Colombo I got off and got on a German passenger freighter, which was a smart new ship. It took me via Calcutta and Singapore into the southern Philippines.

Going back a little bit, I went through several military museums in Germany which were extraordinary things to me. I was made well aware of the Nazi influence in Germany which, at the time, was prominent everywhere. Big maps throughout middle Europe were used as posters to argue about the boundarychanges that had been made by World War I which weren't working out. An extraordinary atmosphere of unrest was obvious to everybody. This was in '34, but the unrest was very evident.

I spent about four days in Palestine where I fell into the hands of the British Navy which I had never known before. They took me under their wing in almost every conceivable way, both aboard and ashore. I spent two days on a British destroyer, the ARDENT, as a guest, although it was in dock at Haifa all the time. I traveled with some British officers up to Jersalem.

This was interesting in those years because the Jews were just then starting to come to Palestine in large numbers and were starting to build the new city of Tel Aviv. They came from all over the world, and I was much impressed by the heterogeneous physiques and color of the Jews and in the architecture that they brought to Tel Aviv from north Germany, from Russia, from Argentina, from the United States, etcetera. There were colonial salt box houses, Moorish castle type houses, things with Russian onions on them, things like that to indicate the polyglot composition of the Jewish population.

On the German freighter I was extraordinarily impressed by the fact that the whole crew had to be indoctrinated in Nazism constantly. There were only about twenty or thirty men in the crew but they had to drill every night from five to seven on deck in a uniform with rifles and give the "Heil Hitler" salute, and goose step up and down the deck. They did that every night, including Sunday nights, for the ten days or so I was on the ship. The captain was an ardent Nazi and tried to indoctrinate me, among others, on how fine the concept was.

In Colombo and Singapore I also got fine treatment through introduction passed along by my naval contacts in Palestine. The British Navy was very nice in showing me all around in Colombo and Singapore, which were eye opening to me. The British were very strong in those years in those areas. There was a lot to be seen that was new to my young eyes.

Miss Kitchen: So you joined the AUGUSTA by going the long way around the world.

Admiral Lee: That's right, but when I ended up out there I found that the AUGUSTA didn't want me but that there was a vacancy on the HERON. So I ended up on the mine sweeper for duty with aircraft, and then went to the AUGUSTA later.

Miss Kitchen: You were telling me an interesting thing while you were with the Asiatic Fleet of your trip to Chungking.

Admiral Lee: Still with the travel bug in me, I got what amounted to about sixteen or seventeen days leave while the AUGUSTA was in Shanghai. We weren't allowed to fly while the ships were in port in China in those years, so I beat my way up to Chungking. Actually I went to Sui Fu, which is about eighty miles above Chungking, which is the equivalent of going up the Mississippi River past Chicago and on up into northern Minnesota. I did this by hitch-hiking various ways.

Part of the way I went on U. S. river gun boats; the PANAY was one of them. Part of the way I went on a commercial oil tanker and part of the way by a little commercial airplane which was a Loening amphibian - a strange type. It had one big float with the passengers inside it, and the pilots sat up in a little tower above their heads. This ran between Shanghai and Chungking.

From Ichang, which is at the foot of the gorges of the Yangtze, to Chungking, I went on a tiny British Imperial Oil Company's gasoline tanker. This went up the rapids of the upper reaches of the Yangtze, and this was about the most interesting trip I ever made in my life. The MONOCACY was the station ship at Chungking, which is way, way up in the interior of China and the sights were all new, extraordinary, edifying, and interesting.

I recall now the movie that has been shown in recent years called "The Sand Pebbles," the nickname of the SAN PABLO, a river gunboat. This was that part of China where in those same years the missionaries were having many troubles in central China. We had troubles with the missionaries, too, in Chefoo, China, which is a port in North China where the HERON spent its summers. The missionaries used Chefoo as a big summer vacation resort for missions scattered all over the interior of China. They had a big vacation resort in Tsingtao, too, where the AUGUSTA usually spent the summer.

We in the Navy had a lot of contacts with the missionaries but we were quite a different sort of people - the young, adventurous, roustabout, Navy crews, and the missionaries, who usually were sedate, elderly, and dedicated people. We often talked with them about why it was necessary to have river gun boats fifteen hundred miles up in the interior of China looking after the interests of the missionaries. This was actually the principal reason we were there. Our commercial interests were very small. Over beers we used to discuss this problem a good deal with the missionaries and among ourselves. I've often thought of it since - a far cry from separation of church and state.

I came down the river on another little boat. Many books have been written about the gorges of the Yangtze, but you have to see them to believe them. The level of the river goes up and down some three hundred feet depending on the rains in the various valleys. The pilots have to know how the channel is going to shift with the rapid rise and fall of the water level.

It was a great lesson in the influence of sea power on history, at least in my young eyes, to see the Chinese junk and what had been done by the junk for China. Through the centuries they had been the cargo carriers in the rivers and canals and along sea coasts of all of China and Indo China. They are very primitive ships whose design has changed practically not at all for centuries. They were awkward and silly to look at, but they did the job just perfectly. I got pretty fascinated with Chinese junks and still am.

When we were based in Chefoo, a friend of mine and I got four or five days off and took a trip to Port Arthur and Dairen, on the northern shore of the Gulf of Pechili in Manchuria. Darien and Port Arthur were the principal Japanese objectives in the Russo-Japanese War. The Russians were very anxious not to have Port Arthur captured and had fortified it very strongly and had a lot of naval installations there. Port Arthur was the destination of the Russian Fleet coming all the way from the Baltic through the Suez and around Africa. They fought the battle of Tsushima Straits near here and all got sunk or captured.

Dairen is a very beautiful city near Port Arthur. Except for Singapore, Port Arthur was the biggest naval base I had seen in the Orient. Even the Japanese in these years had not gone to the lengths the Russians had thirty years before in building up a big base for their navy in the far western Pacific. There were big casemates with twelve or fourteen inch cannons, similar to what we had on the big battleships. The evidences of Russian architecture and the Russian influence in the area were of interest to us, little realizing that we were looking at a vignette of another phase of naval history in a period which was only about thirty years before our time out there.

I got the same sort of a deal from the Navy Department going back to duty at Pensacola, Florida, from the western Pacific. I was allowed to go on my own with leave and travel time, which gave me about two months as I recall.

I did this one by getting on a Japanese freighter which took me from Manila down through Singapore and then down the east coast of Africa. We hit just about every port from Zanzibar down around the Cape of Good Hope. It was a Japanese freighter, but it carried eight passengers. It was pretty ancient, but the trip was interesting. All the passengers but me got off the ship in Colombo - they were Britishers. From Colombo, around Africa, and over to South America, I was the only Anglo-Saxon on the ship.

I got off and went across south Africa by railroad from Lourenco Marques in Portuguese East Africa to Johannesburg, and then down to Durban where I rejoined the freighter. We went to Capetown and then across the South Atlantic to Sao Paulo in Brazil. There I got on Pan American Airways and flew with several overnight stops up to Miami.

The time on the Jap freighter was valauble in that I got a good indoctrination in Japanese customs. After all the foreign passengers left the ship there were many long days at sea. We lived on canned Japanese food exclusively, and that's almost a starvation diet for any Anglo- Saxon. I played chess and the Japanese game of "Go" which is something like chess for endless hours with the skipper - he trying to teach me "Go" and beating me easily at both chess and "Go." I never could learn much about "Go" - it's much harder than chess. He spoke pretty good English, one of the few that did, and we had many diverting hours together. He liked his whiskey and I learned a lot about Japanese philosophy from him.

Miss Kitchen: Did that help you in the future, do you think? When you speak of learning Japanese philosophy - were you saying that seriously?

Admiral Lee: I'm not talking about deep philosophy, I'm just talking about the Japanese way of life and the Japanese way of thinking.

He liked to reminisce about his youth and things of that sort. We had weeks to do it in, just us two, and I learned a lot about him and about Japan. I used to tell him about my life traveling around. I think we both enjoyed it, but whether or not it was any use to me I don't know. It was a friendship, and I enjoyed it. I think I learned more about Japanese character from him than I did in many travels throughout Japan.

Miss Kitchen: Then you went to Pensacola as flight instructor?

Admiral Lee: Yes. I served almost two years there. For a while I was the assistant to the Chief of Flight Training, who was Commander Gerald Bogan. In my second year I became the chief flight instructor in Squadron Five, which was the fighter airplane type of training. It was fun and I enjoyed it.

We lived a very pleasant life in those years with never a care and lots of good fun - met lots of nice people. I met for the first time the girl I subsequently married several years later. Her name was then Harriet Davis Tyler and she was married to one of my flight students. Subsequently I was married and divorced and she was widowed, and we were married in the middle of World War II by proxy.

Miss Kitchen: I'm going to getto that. I don't want to get to that out of context.

1 Lee - 47

Do you have any stories about Admiral Bogan or Admiral Halsey in those days?

Admiral Lee: I suppose that no one who has ever served with Admiral Bogan or Admiral Halsey lacks stories about them because they are pretty good generators of stories. I don't know any that I can recall other than the one I mentioned with Halsey as a fellow flight student. I have great admiration for both of those gentlemen. They are the type of person who is so necessary in military leadership in war and times of stress and strain - when a job needs to be done no matter what it costs. They had great personal magnetism and leadership and anybody would go to hell for them any time they asked them to. They didn't do so well in the peace years when things are administrative, bundled in red tape, and bureaucracy prevails. They were impatient with it. They are one of the two types that it takes to run a Navy through decades of both war and peace. But they are wonderful exponents of the leader-in-war type.

Miss Kitchen: And they were both picturesque.

Admiral Lee: Picturesque and colorful.

Miss Kitchen: You were fortunate in serving with both of them I should think.

Admiral Lee: I think I was.

Miss Kitchen: Then you went aboard the carrier ENTERPRISE.

Admiral Lee: Yes. I went back to Fighting Squadron Six, as it was called then. It was the same Red Rippers under a different number. We made the shakedown cruise of the ENTERPRISE to Rio. We were in our hey-day as young fliers and there's nothing more that the Brazilians like than daredevil flying. We had a very pleasant week in Rio - a nice time going down and back.

The ENTERPRISE was a new ship and one of the first built from the ground up as a carrier. We were all thrilled with it. I recall that my squadron, under the leadership of a fine squadron commander, led the ship into port with a flying display and flew up the entire length of the Avenida Rio Branco which is the principal street of Rio, some of us below the level of the buildings on each side, and flathatted on every beach in Rio scattering the swimmers by thousands. The Brazilians thought it was wonderful. "Bravo" was the word. One doesn't do that anymore.

Miss Kitchen: Who was your commanding officer?

Admiral Lee: Ralph Jennings, of the Red Rippers. The executive officer, who was one of the principal leading lights, was Tommy (Red) Tomlinson. Both of them should have been flying in Rickenbacker days to have been at their apogee.

I had about seven or eight months on the ENTERPRISE. Admiral Halsey was our admiral on board. We had many interesting times in the West Indies.

I was transferred, to my great regret at the time, to be the executive officer of Scouting Squadron Five attached to the carrier YORKTOWN, a sister ship. I served in the YORKTOWN for about a year. We came back to the West Coast and our squadron was based in San Diego with the ship in Long Beach. I don't remember any events of very great interest at the time.

We were all conscious of the fact that war was coming closer in the world. We felt that it would come and we knew that we would have trouble with Japan. We were interested in the Japanese developments but mostly we went our carefree way. We had war games attacking Pearl Harbor again, and the Panama Canal again.

Miss Kitchen: Your next duty, I'm quoting you, was out of the Navy. However, I know it was extremely interesting, and I'd like to have you tell me about that.

Admiral Lee: I was told that I would be ordered to Venezuela for duty as Naval Attache. I hit the overhead and tried to get out of it like mad, but didn't succeed. I was sent to Venezuela because President Roosevelt had decided that our ambassadorial and diplomatic representation in South America was entirely inadequate for the development of his Alliance of the Americas. He was astounded that many embassies in Latin America had no military attaches in them, so he ordered that all those billets be filled at once. I was one victim.

I was first accredited to Colombia and Venezuela, then the office was separated and I became just Venezuela with residence in Caracas. I was there for almost three years. In the last year I was accredited also as Naval Attache to the Netherlands, West Indies, mostly Curacao and Aruba, which are just off the Venezualan coast.

Venezuela had practically no Navy and the country was the victim of having been under almost thirty years of dictatorship by a very tyranical dictator known as Gomez, the Tyrant of the Andes. He was ruthless and cruel. The principal industry of Venezuela was the oil business. There were about five thousand Americans in Venezuela, about two thousand in Caracas, about ninety-five percent of them connected with the oil business in one way or another, or industries working with it.

Although I was the naval attache, I worked mostly with anything in the embassy that was of interest to the ambassador.

These were the years when World War II had started in Europe, and the Nazis were penetrating South America. The Nazis were running a big Colombian air line, based in Colombia but covering northern South America, and were using it as a base for clandestine work. We were very interested in this penetration.

The United States at that time did not permit any agent of the FBI to work outside of the continental United States, so I was given a sub rosa commission in the FBI to be an agent for them, working mostly on this Nazi business. This was by no means my full time work, but I did have a considerable amount of interest in it and put much time on it.

In the last six months that I was there, Washington sent down an FBI agent, who was not admitted to be such, to be my assistant. He took over most of the work. It was interesting and concerned largely with the identification and monitoring of their radio networks. They had clandestine radio stations. We had monitoring equipment. I also had the only amphibian airplane around the place, which could fly almost anywhere landing on rivers in the interior. So I did an awful lot of flying in connection with the investigation of suspicious things and people.

We were not highly successful, but we were fairly successful in penetrating a lot of it. We knew who most the people were. We were monitoring their programs on machines which I had nothing to do with, which was done by another department.

We were active in watching the pilots and what they were doing on this line,— they were all Nazi Germans — what they were interested in, and what they were trying to get.

Miss Kitchen: This was the airline?

Admiral Lee: Yes, the Colombian airline which was run by Nazi Germans entirely. It was a Germany company hired by the Colombian government to run their national air lines. It covered Peru, Colombia, Equador, Panama, Central America, Venezuela. This was interesting and all sub rosa at the time. It was never known to anybody outside the embassy that I was doing this.

Miss Kitchen: How did you go about it?

Admiral Lee: It's purely being the receiving end of leads from Washington or elsewhere saying investigate this, investigate that, who is this person, what is he doing? Getting agents to work for us in that area who were better positioned to deal with it than we were. There was quite a large German colony in northern South America of refugees from Hitler's Germany, many of them Jewish, whom we were able to use effectively, as can be well imagined.

The second helpful thing was that during the Spanish Civil War a large number of Basques from Spain had sailed across the ocean. In fact the fishing industry almost as a whole had come across the ocean to Venezuela - the famous oceanic fishing industry of the Basques had just sailed in their tiny fishing boats, with their familes on board. So there was quite a large colony of Basques in Venezuela. They started the fishing business in Venezuela, or rather started a new and vigorous one where there had been nothing but a sort of pastoral type of fishing beforehand. The Basques were very effective. They got around everywhere in the coastal ports all the time and knew everybody in the shipping business. They became a very profitable group for us to know, and I became sort of their agent in the embassy.

As a matter of fact, I got started in this because I was anxious to improve my Spanish, and living about a thirty-five minute drive out of the city I hired as my chauffeur a Basque refugee who was a PhD professor in philosophy at the University of Bilbao. He drove me back and forth to work and elsewhere. I used to translate articles in the READER'S DIGEST into Spanish as we drove and he would correct me and find the words for me, although he couldn't speak any English. It was effective, two years of it, in helping my Spanish.

With these means we were able to keep track of what was going on quite effectively, and as far as I knew and others knew our particular activities were never known to the German airlines, which went out of business when Pearl Harbor occurred.

Miss Kitchen: Do you remember any instances of espionage that you can tell?

Admiral Lee: No. It wasn't that kind of espionage, in a way. It was mostly a collation of all the intelligence that you could get which would divulge their plans, operations, aims, efforts, and so on.

We were very much afraid that this particular group would undertake, in case of World War, to damage the Panama Canal. Begin adjacent in Colombia they were in a good position to do so, so we were most active in looking into anything that they tried to do about getting information about Panama.

There was no particular type of thing, other than locating by triangulation methods the location of their secret radios. They were broadcasting Nazi propaganda from clandestine stations that the Colombian and Venezuelan governments weren't very adept at locating. We were able to put them into a very small area and then turn the job of finding them over to the local governments, and they were able to stop them, which they wanted to do. There was not very much cloak and dagger work. It was routine investigation of this, that, and the other - sub rosa but not with any secret inks or any type of —

#1 Lee - 55

Miss Kitchen: Did you feel that you made a contribution by the information you were able to turn over?

Admiral Lee: Oh, I'm sure we did. We were able to assist the Venezuelan government and other governments in stopping this clanestine radio propagandizing, which they were doing, and which the governments were anxious to suppress. We found out that there was an organization. We didn't know exactly what it's plans were. We knew that they were planning to do something in the event of a world wide eruption of hostilities, which in those years was envisaged as something which might happen, and we had most of them pin-pointed and knew where they lived, and we had given this information to the governments concerned. They knew that if anything happened they could put their hands on practically everyone of them and all their families instantly.

Miss Kitchen: Everyone who would be subversive?

Admiral Lee: Yes.

Miss Kitchen: Did you have any incidents with submarines in that part of the world?

Admiral Lee: Yes, I did. This mostly occurred in my last months in Venezuela.

The attack on Pearl Harbor occurred six months before I left. In the year before that international affairs in the military and diplomatic worlds were very touch and go. We were all conscious of the fact that the United States was probably going to be sucked into World War II. Additionally, the battle of Britain was being fought, the war was going on in Europe, and almost a hundred percent of the high octane gasoline which was used in the battle of Britain came from Lake Maracaibo via Aruba and Curacao. The Nazis had sent submarines into this area – they actually attacked the small oil tankers which were used to take the crude oil out of Lake Maracaibo. There were only twelve of these critically important, specially built, shallow draft tankers in the world. Sinking them would greatly handicap getting oil to the big oil refineries in Curacao and Aruba. Big tankers came in and took the refined and crude oil to Europe. There were several Nazi submarine attacks against these very important tankers. Not only that, but the subs made some attacks against the shore installations. I pursued this matter in later years to find out what actually happened.

On the coast of the Island of Aruba, near the refinery, is a semi-circular, almost land locked bay, called Bullen Bay. It is sort of like the inside of an inverted cone or a crater of a volcano, sloping hillsides going up smoothly all around from the water's edge. These sloping hillsides were covered almost completely by gasoline storage tanks. When you looked at them, practically all you could see was tanks and very little land in between. These were the storage tanks for the gasoline and other petroleum products going to Europe to sustain the allies in the war.

A Nazi submarine got into Bullen Bay one day and fired seven shots into these tanks. To anybody who examined the scene, as I had, it was the world's greatest miracle that it didn't start the whole thing up in one of the world's largest conflagrations. Three of the tanks were pierced by the submarine's small cannon shells, going in one side and out the other side of the tank, but each tank was almost empty at the time and the gasoline was not ignited. One tank actually caught fire but there was so little gasoline left in it that it didn't get a chance to burn much and they were able to put it out. The rest of them landed in what were the almost hard to find areas of ground that you could hit without hitting a tank. If the sub had fired about five more shots it seems that it would have been inevitable that there would have been a holocaust.

In later years after the war I located the records of the German skipper to find out why he had submerged right away and gone without doing a better job. Was he out of amunition or what? It developed that he was convinced that he was under attack by airplanes and that he thought he would be sunk if he didn't go. We know for a positive fact from investigation everywhere in the area that there was no airplane within fifty miles of him.

Miss Kitchen: He gave that just as an excuse?

Admiral Lee: We don't know, but he thought he had a report of an attacking airplane so he made a crash dive and left. However, other submarines did sink some of these small very valuable tankers, some of which were under the Venezuelan flag and some under the British flag. They only sank the British flag ships, but they damaged one neutral Venezuelan flag which was something of an international incident, but which was papered over.

When all these things were going on, another task I had as naval attache caused a lot of headaches. I was what is known as the Naval Control of Shipping Officer for the whole north coast of South America. This is a war time measure for the control of merchant shipping, and involves keeping track of every merchant ship on the seas. You have to have a departure report and an arrival report for all ships going into and leaving port. It has to be sent and in code in war time, and it permits a central control authority to keep track of the ships all over the oceans of the world. This was a poorly developed thing along the northern coast of South America in 1939 and '40. As can well be imagined, there were other places which were thought to be much more important.

In Venezuela it was being done by consular agents or somebody in a grocery store that we hired on a pick-up basis - not quite that bad - but we just found some white Anglo-Saxon somewhere in a little port and said, "Will you be our agent for this purpose?" This was working fine (we didn't pay them anything) within limits until things started to get tense and we found it was all full of bugs. They didn't know how to use any codes well, and I had a tremendous job trying to get this ship reporting thing going with reliable agents trained well enough in each one of the ports. In retrospect, I should have started on this in the first week I was there, but I didn't learn about it until I had been there over a year and a half practically. But this became a big item handled on a crash basis.

As things got more tense I was also made part of a task force centered on Panama for the defense of the Panama Canal in connection with submarine activity, the tankers mostly, in the Caribbean.

Immediately adjacent to Venezuela on it's northeastern tip is the island of Trinidad. The island of Trinidad and the coast of Venezuela enclose an almost square, practically land locked, bay which is about twenty or thirty miles on a side. There are only two very narrow entrances. This is the Gulf of Paria, and it became of great significance to us early in the war because it was about the only place around there that could be used as an absolutely submarine proof harbor.

If we could close both the entrances, we could let our own ships in and they would be free from submarine attack. But we had to arrange for the complete cooperation of neutral Venzuela. This took a good deal of doing because the Venezuelans wanted to stay neutral, although willing to be neutral on our side. But they were very meticulous. It was touchy, and I was the agent.

We had previously started a naval air station in Trinidad. Admiral Radford had started it as a part of the destroyers for bases deal. Admiral Reagan was the chief man there when this was going on. Very early, before we got into the war, if you flew over the Gulf of Paria or went through it in a small boat you would see in the harbor of Port of Spain, capitol of Trinidad, literally dozens and dozens of badly damaged merchant ships that had sailed or been towed into the Gulf of Paria. They had been damaged by torpedo attacks from Nazi submarines attacking the shipping lanes from South America to North America. This was their refuge and repair spot, and you could see many tankers and cargo ships, often with a big list or down by the bow or stern, and with great gaping holes in their sides from torpedo damage. We had to set up repair facilities there and fix them up before they could go on again.

So many of my associations with the Venezuelans had to do with the use of Paria for these purposes and with their letting us close the entrances in their territorial waters.

We had to put detection devices in them and check that they working without letting the Venezuelans know too much about it, so to speak, so that they could say they were still neutral. But they were very cooperative and it worked well.

It was a tremendously valuable place for us in all the war for the shakedown training of our own Navy ships in a place which was absolutely secure from submarine attack. We made all our shakedown cruises for carriers down there. I went down later in the war when the ESSEX went into commission and started our flight operations right in that same place. I was then Air Officer of the ESSEX.

Miss Kitchen: With whom did you deal in these negotiations?

Admiral Lee: A great many people, basically the Ambassador and the Foreign Minister. I worked with the Minister of Defense of Venezuela and the head of the Navy, and the head of what they called their Coastal Service, which was a sort of port director system for their own towns, and with the corresponding officials in Trinidad, which was then under the British flag, also with our overall defense headquarters in San Juan, Puerto Rico and in Panama.

Miss Kitchen: Who was the ambassador in Venezuela at the time?

Admiral Lee: His name was Frank Corrigan. He was an unusual man - originally a surgeon for the United Fruit Company in San Juan, Costa Rica. When Roosevelt said that every Latin American legation should be raised to embassy status there was only a legation in Costa Rica. Roosevelt was hunting for an ambassador to send to Costa Rica, and when he got no name right away because State said they hadn't been able to find a name he said, "Why don't you ask the people in Costa Rica who they'd like to have to be ambassador?" So they did, and they said, "We'd like to have Dr. Corrigan. He's the most respected American citizen in Costa Rica and we all know him well. Why don't you make him ambassador?" So they did, and that started him on a long ambassadorial career which went from Costa Rica to Salvador, to Panama, then Venezuela, and then up to the United Nations where he ended his career.

Miss Kitchen: When you say "Dr." do you mean M.D.?

Admiral Lee: Yes, he was a surgeon for the United Fruit Company.

I might turn now to leaving Venezuela. We had no facilities for looking after our small amphibious plane in Caracas, so about every three months I would fly over to Panama where we had a big air station and I could get it serviced, make engine changes and repairs. On the day of the attack on Pearl

Harbor I was in Panama doing just that. I was living with the Operations Officer in his room in BOQ of the Coco Solo Naval Air Station at Colon on the Atlantic side of the Canal. He'd gone out to play golf on a Sunday morning and I was lying on my bunk at about two o'clock in the afternoon, when a seaman came in from the COD's office and said he had to find the Operations Officer because the Japanese were going to attack Panama. I said, "Let's get this straight" - or words to that effect. It took him a long time to convince me. In the end I called up the COD to find out what he was talking about. He said it was true that they had attacked Pearl Harbor and there was a suspicion that they might attack Panama, and they had to find the Operations Officer. So I gave the messenger the keys to the Operations Officer's car, which he had left with me because he went out to play golf in his golf partner's car. I told him to go out to the Gatun Dam golf course and drive the car around on the course until he found the Operations Officer and get him back, which he eventually did. I didn't think the messenger believed any of this either, and I wasn't sure I did, and many others didn't know whether we were being duped by some practical joke - anyway it was in the back of our minds for a while.

Needless to say, all of this started a considerable amount of confusion in Panama. There were reports that there were three Japanese task forces at sea - one had hit Pearl Harbor, one was due to hit the West Coast, and one was due to hit

Panama, and probably all simultaneously arranged, so Panama could expect theirs at any moment. This is all we had to go on and we couldn't disput that it might be true, so we went all out.

Panama had had several drill blackouts prior to this in preparation for the real thing, but they had been very ineffective. The commanding general of the Army, whose responsibility it was, was very peeved with Panamanians – they wouldn't turn out their lights at night and most of them had kerosene lanterns and candles in shacks with no telephones or radio anyway, so it was almost impossible to make it work. But we went into a blackout situation which, when evening came, wasn't very good. The commanding general got awfully mad and was doing everything he could to make the blackout perfect. Blackouts have always been somewhat doubtful in my mind. In any event he finally decided in desperation to pull the main power switches that furnished the electricity to the entire city, and this he did. This started one of the most awful pandemoniums ever, because nobody could use telephones and nobody knew what to do. Some of the canal locks were caught with the power off and the lock gates half open with water spilling out. The anti-aircraft batteries had emergency sources of power and they were able to function, but nobody could communicate on any land lines that were supplied by city electricity. For several hours there was no way for the commanding general himself

1 Lee - 65

of getting to know what the magnitude of the problem was. He just didn't realize it. He thought things were working pretty well because everything was black.

Well, it wasn't working very well. Everybody got out into the streets. People were smashing each other's headlights when a headlight was turned on by someone trying to drive a car. There was no power for radio broadcasts. It was real pandemonium for awhile - kind of disgraceful when you look back, but that's what happened from my point of observation.

Miss Kitchen: People got scared.

Admiral Lee: Yes, and there was always the feeling that at any moment an attack might come.

Miss Kitchen: The whole West Coast had those rumors, and logically so.

Admiral Lee: Yes. Well in Panama - I only saw the Atlantic end, Coco Solo, but Coco Solo was pretty darned messy.

Anyway we finally got through the first day or so, and I wanted to get back to Venezuela. I knew there would be a crisis in my office. They wouldn't let me go, because they said that they were going to shoot at any airplane that flew anywhere and I'd be shot down. Also I was having an engine changed. They stopped all work on that and on anything except what they thought was being gotten ready to fight Japs with. So my mechanic and I finished putting the engine back together - mostly my mechanic I must say. We got it all set to go, but it was not until four days later that I was allowed to leave Panama.

So I flew back to Maracay, the place where I kept my airplane in Venezuela. It is a small town about two and a half hours from Caracas over the most terrible, twisty, tortuous mountain road anybody ever drove. Very few people would do it willingly at any time, but that's where I had to keep my airplane.

When I arrived at Maracay, I was astounded to see the ambassador and about eight other officials of the Venezuelan government, and what not, waiting for me to come in. It developed that when everything happened about America going to war no messages got through into the embassy at all from anybody in Washington. They couldn't even communicate with them. They didn't know what to do or what instructions the ambassador had. They were going on hearsay, and it was terrible. The reason I became important was there was only one message from Washington in the Embassy - it was in code for me from the Navy Department and I was the only one that could decode the message.

We got in cars and went tearing up this awful road which practically made you seasick if you went more than thirty miles an hour.

There is no page 67.

We got to the embassy and I had to go into my little dark closet with my secret coding maching and decode the message. When I came out I read the very brief message, "Rainbow five in effect." The ambassador said, "What does Rainbow five mean?" and I said, "I don't know." So we were no better off than before except that we knew that Rainbow five was in effect.

Rainbow five was the emergency war plan of the United States, which meant it included the color plans of various nations and areas. Rainbow five meant it's the works — we are at war with Japan and Europe together, the United States is at war — carry your war plan into effect.

Actually there were no steps of any great significance that I or anybody else was to take in Venezuela at the time. We were a back water from war so it meant little, but it was an interesting episode. The whole city was waiting for the naval attache to come down and give them the straight dope, and he could give them nothing.

Miss Kitchen: Did you know the United States was at war? You knew that from Panama.

Admiral Lee: Oh yes, we knew that from radio broadcasts. We heard the news broadcasts that were all over the air. We knew we were at war, and knew what was going on.

1 Lee - 69

The U. S. government represented in Panama by the ambassador and his staff, of which I was one, were the sole representatives of the U. S. government in Venezuela. All the oil companies wondered what are we doing now, what's going to happen next? They were very anxious to have somebody tell them what to do. Shall we send these tankers out?

Miss Kitchen: What did you tell them to do?

Admiral Lee: We said to keep on doing business as usual. We don't know anything different. We can't stop everything here. The World War is going to go on in much more important ways and other places, and to have everything grind to a halt here isn't going to help it.

Miss Kitchen: And the tankers were needed no less on an emergency basis than before.

Admiral Lee: Yes. Well, it all got cleared up eventually.
When we got into the war my relationship with the Dutch and the shipping people became clarified. Our plans were all right and things went smoothly. These submarine attacks occurred before we got in the war.

Miss Kitchen: Did they continue?

Admiral Lee: No, they didn't continue, I don't know why. The Nazi submarines were starting to get discouraged in that area. As I recall we didn't have any direct submarine contacts in our area of responsibility after that.

My years in Venezuela were very pleasant ones.

Miss Kitchen: Were you still a bachelor at this time?

Admiral Lee: No. I was married just before I left for Venezuela. My wife was down there with me.

The country is an extremely interesting one and I was free to fly all over southern South America. The Orinoco Valley lies largely in Venezuela and it's one of the largest river systems in the world. On all the maps available to me very large splotches of it were marked simply "unexplored." Many explorers were interested in it and I took some of them on flights down into the area, flying where nobody but the native indians had ever been before.

Miss Kitchen: Did you ever land in unexplored territory?

Admiral Lee: I landed in many places in the Oronoco and Amazon Rivers in an amphibian airplane. The rivers, of course, had been explored. I had to go down and find explorers that got lost - impossible to do, but we'd go down and make the search.

At that time there was a Venezuelan-Brazilian Border Commission that had been working for fifteen years trying to define the border between Venezuela and Brazil, which was described in their earliest treaties as the water shed between the Amazon and Oronoco Rivers. Well, it's nothing but jungle and they were trying to establish where the actual water shed was. This was accomplished by making some photographic markers with piles of white stones that could be seen from the air in various places, then triangulating from these bases and trying to work it out. Since I had the only airplane that could land in the rivers, I was constantly being made available to them by our ambassador to help them out in some phases of this exploration. It was extremely interesting.

Miss Kitchen: Wasn't it dangerous?

Admiral Lee: Yes, in retrospect. My little airplane only went about one hundred and forty miles an hour but I could fly for five hours right over the tops of trees in the jungle and it would be just like flying over the ocean. That's all you saw was tops of trees for five hours straight without changing course, and that was as much gasoline as I had.

Miss Kitchen: Did you ever find any of these explorers who were lost?

Admiral Lee: Yes. We had places where we could go where the Indian tribes had a system of reporting, more or less, and we could go down and ask them. I would take a Venezuelan government representative down.

There was a famous character named Jimmy Angel, who was known all over northern South America and Central America as an explorer. He discovered and named Angel Falls which were then, and are today, the highest waterfalls in the world. They are in Venezuela. He was always exploring in that area and then he would be unreported for several weeks. His family lived in Caracas or Bogota half the time and they would call on me to go down and see whether or not there was any evidence of where he was, and whether he was lost. So I did. I saw several Indian villages just out of the stone age. They had some little barnstorming airplane types that would go down and drop bolts of cloth to the Indian villages. In exchange for these bolts of cloth the Indians would go down to a place where there was a sand bar in the river and leave messages for us.

Miss Kitchen: Did you ever have any close calls?

Admiral Lee: No. I had a lot of interesting experiences, but no dangerous ones.

Miss Kitchen: So your interesting tour in Venezuela came to an end.

Admiral Lee: I finally got out about six months after Pearl Harbor, actually in May of '42. I was ordered to be the flag secretary of Admiral Fitch, who was then embarked in the HORNET in the western Pacific. After a short period in Washington, I left for the western Pacific and got to Pearl Harbor where I found on arrival that the day beforehand the HORNET had been sunk and Admiral Fitch was believed to be alive, but they weren't sure. The rest of the staff was going to be coming back to Pearl Harbor, and they would decide by the time they got back what would be done. The end product was that that particular staff was then disbanded, and I was put on the staff of COMAIRPAC, then headquartered in Pearl Harbor.

I was assigned as the flag secretary and I stayed only for a period of about three or four months. The principal thing that happened at that time was the Battle of Midway which took place fairly close to Pearl Harbor and in which we were all very intensely interested. Through reading Japanese codes we knew of the events that were leading up to it, as has been subsequently divulged. We knew from the codes that the Japs were going to attack Midway and all the planned maneuvers for running the American side of the battle was being done in the office of Admiral Nimitz in Pearl Harbor. So every development of it was close to us. Being on the staff of the Commander, Air Craft, Pacific Fleet, which was the unit principally concerned in it, it was a very exciting time for us. I was only in on the fringes of it. I had no direct part in that planning other than to know it was going on and to watch some units coming back - planes that went out from Pearl Harbor itself and would come back and tell us of what was happening.

It was one of the decisive battles of history, without question, and I think most of us were mindful of the fact at the time. We were all keyed up. I can remember spending all night up, one of the nights of the battle, when there was no reason for me being up all night at all. We just never went to sleep because we were afraid that we would miss some development. But it was on the periphery of my responsibilities.

We were very irritated by the great effort of the Army Air Corps to take part in the Battle of Midway. They did participate to some degree which didn't pay off very well in military accomplishment of any significance. There was a large Army Air Corps installation at Hickham Field adjacent to Pearl Harbor. So we were mindful of the fact that they weren't going to overlook any opportunity to participate in it if they could.

Miss Kitchen: Did you have any dealings with Admiral Nimitz during this period?

Admiral Lee: Yes. Only because of the fact that I would frequently go over to his intelligence conferences as a member of the staff of COMAIRPAC, and he would come over and see us every once in awhile. Admiral Spruance had been in and out a great deal. He was the one in command of our forces afloat at Midway. I was seeing them socially often from a more or less lower level. I had little or no offical business with them at all.

Miss Kitchen: Did you have any anecdotes or episodes to relate or any recollections of Admiral Nimitz?

Admiral Lee: I've had a lot of recollections of Admiral Nimitz through the years. As I say, I knew him as my skipper in the Asiatic Fleet, and I've always been a great admirer of him. I think he's one of the very best men I've ever known. He was not a soft spoken man, when he wanted to get things done. He was a hard driving man and if you didn't get the job done, you knew it from him, but kindly and tactfully. For the most part, he was one of the most genial, gentlemanly, soft spoken, suave people I have ever known. Socially he was all of those things, but he coupled that with a force of character that made him get things done which the glad-hander with everybody doesn't get done. The latter sometimes gets ahead if nothing important has to be gotten done. Admiral Nimitz had the hard driving quality that distinguished both him and Admiral King. I thought King had the same quality but without Admiral Nimitz' pleasant social accomplishments to go with it. I worked for both of them.

Miss Kitchen: Would that have been at a later date with Admiral King?

Admiral Lee: No. Admiral King was the skipper of the LEXINGTON when I was on it. He was a very determined man. He was quite correct when he told the press that when the things got tough they sent for a son of a bitch, and that's why he got to be CNO.

He was my skipper in one of the Fleet maneuvers in which we attacked Panama (it may have been Hawaii). Anyway, we were supposed to attack a big shore base in a Fleet maneuver. I was in Fighting Squadron Five and I had the number two plane position in an eighteen plane squadron. The skipper took off first and then the number two plane took off and then the number three, et cetera. They were arranged on the deck in that way. These were little stick and wire airplanes, very light, and we only had about seventy-five feet of deck to take off in. Men worked all night getting the planes parked ready for take-off in this order. The bow of the LEXINGTON was not like the square bows that you have in the modern carrier, it was more rounded and came to sort of a blunt rounded point, so it meant the closer you got to the bow the fewer airplanes you could get on it. The skipper took off in the early dawn on this very important attack on this shore base - the first attack of this big Fleet maneuver. Lieutenant Lee's plane was number two, and after the initial warm-up the engine quit and wouldn't get started again. Nobody else could move until Lee got going again, because you'd have to unstack the whole lot of airplanes which would take hours and hours. Or you could push it over the side without any further ado. In a war I guess you would have. The flight deck officer came, the boatswain's mate came, and they wound up my airplane with a hand crank, as you had to do in the days of the inertia starter, and still it wouldn't work. Then they got the engineering experts and still they couldn't make it start. The flight deck officer got in the cockpit and I got out, it didn't work, and I got back in the cockpit and they got some more experts to crank it up, it didn't work. King's boiling point, which was normally low, early in this mess had become very manifest to all hands on board. It ended up with Admiral King coming down and personally cranking up the airplane to show us how it could be done, and still it didn't start. We had to unscramble all the airplanes, and the sun was well up when the first plane took off.

Miss Kitchen: Did you ever find out what was wrong with it?

Admiral Lee: Yes, there was a broken valve inside the engine.

Miss Kitchen: How did Lieutenant Lee feel during this time?

Admiral Lee: Not well. There was nothing I could do and nothing anybody else could do apparently, but it was extremely surprising to me to look up and suddenly find that the skipper was winding the crank. These were very hard to turn over and you couldn't do it more than a couple of times without getting exhausted, so we had relays of them cranking up the airplane.

Miss Kitchen: Was he an admiral then?

Admiral Lee: No, he was the captain of the ship. He never was vindictive about it afterwards. It was just fate. He bawled me out for not having checked it out better beforehand but I think it happened at the time they first tried to start it. Anyway, he was never mad about it afterwards and chalked it up to just one of those things. Very few skippers would have come down and did what he did.

Miss Kitchen: I wanted you to tell the anecdote about Admiral Nimitz' detachment from the AUGUSTA.

Admiral Lee: The AUGUSTA was tied up to buoys in the Whangpoo River, which is a short arm of the Yangtze River in the city of Shanghai. There was a string of mooring buoys up the river and ships tied up bow and stern to these. On the occasion of his detachment and our getting a new skipper, the change of command ceremony took place on the ship. In those days we had full dress uniforms that consisted of dress frock coats that went down to your knees, brass buttons and large heavy gold epaulets, cocked hats, swords with a lot of braid on them, and we all had to be in this outfit for the ceremony. Then in the tradition of the old Navy, Admiral Nimitz went down the gang way after relinquishing command to his successor, Captain Felix Xerxes Gygax, and the boat crew, by tradition, was manned by the junior officers of the ship all in their full dress uniform. So we were in the lifeboat waiting for Admiral Nimitz. He got in and this gaily caparisoned crew rowed him upstream against the current to a Dollar Line steamer which he was getting on with Mrs. Nimitz to go back to the United States. This was all very colorful and all the Sampan coolies and the Chinese for boats and boats around were astounded that this was happening and couldn't figure out how foolish the Americans could be to do anything like this - it looked demeaning to them, I think - but the most demeaning thing was that we weren't in very good condition and the current was very strong, and we got pooped out about three times before we could get to the gangway of the Dollar Line ship, and we just barely made it by the last few strokes of the few people still able to row. Most of us thought we never were going to make it, and we'd drift back down stream, and it would be one of the episodes of history that would never be forgotten. But with Nimitz's encouragements we got there finally. Everybody was giving encouragement to everyone else hoping we would make it.

Miss Kitchen: Was that a tribute to how the crew felt about him, or was that tradition?

Admiral Lee: No, that was a tradition that had been inherited from the British - it was always done. But it was not often in a place where you have a big current that you'd have to row him against which is a little bit beyond the capacity of the non-conditioned crew of rowers.

Miss Kitchen: The incident with Admiral King was back in 1927 or '28?

Admiral Lee: 1930.

Miss Kitchen: This was when you were aboard the LEXINGTON?

Admiral Lee: Yes.

Miss Kitchen: Do you have any other recollections of that time that you were in Pearl?

Admiral Lee: None in particular. It was the first year of the war and Pearl was a terrifically busy place and everybody was working their heads off. The city of Honolulu was blacked out every night. Life was unsociable and not so good. There was scarcely any air conditioning and everybody that had lights on had to have black curtains over the windows. This made it impossible to breathe or live in comfort. It wasn't too pleasant from many points of view but life in Hawaii is always rather gay and pleasant in others.

I was working the whole time to get myself on a ship to go out and fight. Here it was eight months of war gone by and I hadn't seen as much as a pistol go off, and I was feeling that I had to do something better. I was promised that I would get assigned a squadron but I quickly became too senior. All the squadron commanders were then getting promoted so fast and I was pormoted so fast. I was initially ordered to command of Air Group Nine which was forming for the carrier ESSEX, then being built. But before the orders could be written they decided they had to go up another notch in rank and job, so I was made the air officer of the ESSEX instead. I went back to Newport News where she was being built and to get her ready for commissioning, which I did.

Miss Kitchen: What was your grade now?

Admiral Lee: I was lieutenant commander still, but very shortly after that I became a commander.

We were in competition with the carrier YORKTOWN, which was supposed to be commissioned three weeks after the ESSEX. The ESSEX had as a skipper Captain "Wu" Duncan, and the skipper of the YORKTOWN was Captain Jocko Clark. Jocko Clark was a great driver, and he was determined that the YORKTOWN would get finished and commissioned, and get out there and be fighting before the ESSEX did. The contest was on. The rivalry was great. We thought that a lot of dishonest things were done to get things provided for the YORKTOWN which should have come to the ESSEX just so we wouldn't get finished in time, but we never were able to prove anything. We did get out first by a week. We sailed out to the Pacific together actually, but we were commissioned a week before they were.

As a side light, I had visited many of the ships in Pearl Harbor that came back with battle damage, talked to the people and crew, seen the dedication of everybody in the war zone. At the Newport News Shipbuilding plant I was air officer due to take charge of everything that the Air Department would use on the ship - the arresting gear, the catapults, all the gear that goes into aviation supply, et cetera - and I was extremely upset by the attitude of the shipbuilding workers. They were on union hours. They knew they weren't going to be drafted. They were swiping materials and selling them to a big scrap organization in town - all kinds of things that shouldn't have been declared scrap. But in the pressure of war things are done - get it done quickly, don't ask questions. I was so upset by the fact that I would go around in the ship while it was being finished and the people who were supposed to be working were sitting there having a cup of coffee and a talk-fest, or napping, especially at night when you had the night shifts. I would talk to some of them once in awhile and say, "Why are you sitting here doing this when people are dying?" I'd get emotional about it. Well, it never did any good. I can remember writing a long letter to the Superintendant of Shipbuilding attached to the Norfolk Shipbuilding and Drydock Corporation make a public complaint, but I never sent it. It was a sour note to me that these men, many men in their thirties, should have been doing better. In many cases, probably they were not working because they were waiting for some part to come or there was another good reason, but when asked about it their attitude was, "Who the deuce are you to ask? You don't like it, go lump it. We're doing our part and you do yours." Kind of a Billy be damned attitude which just killed me. Nothing ever came of it, and we got the ship in commission. I'm sure it was only a minority of them that did it. It left a bad taste in my mouth. Others who had been in the war zone felt as I did. It was one of the side lights on human beings as human beings.

The ESSEX was commissioned on the thirtieth of December, 1943, as I recall, the day before New Year's Day, so we would get commissioned in that calendar year. An amusing but tragic episode occurred just before the commissioning. I had the watch on board ship and we had a very green crew who had just moved aboard. We had a very elaborate aparatus for flooding the hangar deck of the ship in case of fires and bomb damage. The hangar was divided into compartments, and there were massive spray systems for making curtains of salt water to screen off a fire and tons of water to douse the location of the fire. This was all controlled from a booth that looked down from the top of the inside of the hangar deck. It was called the conflagration station. On the mid watch we had a big sailor up in the conflagration station. He was sitting in front of a big battery of long valve handles which controlled all the water. The telephone at one end of the booth rang, and he had to go along this line of valve handles in order to answer it. He lurched along and his fanny swung against about eight of these valves. It was about two o'clock of a December morning, very, very cold, and with all of the ship's company sound asleep. Thousands of tons of water were let loose in the hangar deck, and went on down into the living spaces below. Well, the confusion was out of this world.

It was a blow and damaged a lot of equipment, and was bad from every point of view. As a public relations effort, it was one of the world's worst. Actually the ship took on so much water that before we could get everything stopped, the ship took a perceptible list. Since the ship was still in the hands of the shipbuilders, it wasn't technically my responsibility, but I certainly shared the blame. If we had had a small skinny man on watch it might never have happened.

The ESSEX went to the Pacific in company with the YORKTOWN. Many of the scenes which were taken in the movie called THE FIGHTING LADY, a famous film about the war episode of the carriers, were taken on the carrier ESSEX by a small photographic team that was going to go out to make such a film. I think they came first to the YORKTOWN, but they spent a lot of time on the ESSEX and many of the scenes of THE FIGHTING LADY (which became the nickname of the YORKTOWN) were actually taken on board the ESSEX. This irritated the ESSEX sailors because the film became known as the story of the YORKTOWN.

Many scenes showed aviators in the ward room and in the pilots ready rooms. The fellows who were doing the photographing were very good. They selected a number of people to portray distinctive personalities. One young officer pilot in one of the ESSEX squadrons was a good looking young fellow. By happenstance he became sort of a featured face in the film, and people remembered him as a principal character in it.

I have to go years ahead now to the surrender ceremony on the MISSOURI in Tokyo Harbor at the end of the war. I was the PIO in charge of it for Admiral Nimitz. Harold Stassen was on Halsey's staff and Stassen had been sent ashore earlier to get some of the early prisoner of war camps open right away and get the prisoners out. He had a radio telephone and was talking to us on the MISSOURI. We heard from some of the press that General MacArthur was going to arrive soon and that he had the liberated General Wainwright with him, plus a couple of colonels and a couple of sargeants, and he was going to bring them all to the ceremony. We thought that wasn't awfully good since there were a lot of naval war prisoners too. So we got on our walkie-talkie to Harold Stassen and said, "We want a senior naval officer and we want a young naval officer, and we want one or two enlisted men out of the prison camps, and we want them down here for this ceremony." The time was short and he had to scramble, but he got some prisoners – a captain, USN, and a young pilot, and a first-class petty officer – and brought the three of them in a little whale boat which got to the MISSOURI's gangway just before the Japanese delegates did. We brought them up so they could be there with Wainwright and the others, giving the naval side of the picture so to speak. The young naval officer who came aboard had no teeth (they had been knocked out by a ball bat in the hands of a Japanese prison guard) but he was cheerful and happy and smiling and almost crying, and so glad was he to be out of prison camp. It turned out that this young pilot was the one featured in THE FIGHTING LADY. Everybody recognized him, but he had never heard of THE FIGHTING LADY, or that he was particularly featured in it, or that he was famous. He couldn't believe it.

Miss Kitchen: At the time the ESSEX got out there, which was early '43, was the time when the shipbuilding effort of the United States was really being felt in the Pacific, and the ESSEX, as you said, and the YORKTOWN, and other ships started out and we began making our march across the Pacific, and although the early days maybe just were strikes, you participated in them. The first incidence that I have as a record of the ESSEX was in September of 1943 against Marcus Island.

Admiral Lee: Yes, this is true. We were the first big carriers to get out of the twenty-four ESSEX class carriers that were built. We had not been able to hit back at the Japs in any significant way until these two carriers arrived. As a sort of a warmup for us, we elected to make a strike at Marcus Island, which was pretty far west in the Pacific, but very isolated and very small and of no very great significance other than the fact the the Japanese had a radio station and a weather station there which was valuable to them. The value of the strike was mostly psychological and for training for us, to make sure that we were operating pretty well. The YORKTOWN and the ESSEX went together. We both struck it. We got practically no opposition but there were anti-aircraft batteries on it. One of our planes that was shot down at Marcus was the young officer I just mentioned who had been in the Japanese prison camp. We thought he had been killed because other pilots said that they saw flames and explosions when his plane hit the ground. We didn't know until we saw him on the MISSOURI that he had survived.

We were pretty exuberant that everything had worked well. The ships were showing themselves to be very fine ships.

I will digress again for history. The technical design of the ESSEX class carriers was in the hands of one man who said what characteristics should be in the ships to make them good aircraft carriers - the aircraft handling arrangements, the aircraft bombing and rearmament arrangements, fueling arrangements, catapulting, arresting gear - all the things that had to do with making them work well in their principal job as the operators of aircraft. This man was in the Bureau of Aeronautics and his name was then Commander J. S. Russell, U. S. Navy. He went on to become a four star officer. He was a man of great vision and ability; he had been on carriers; he knew them; he insisted on getting things done that he felt were necessary, and getting them done in the face of opposition from other people who wanted other things done which would have impaired their efficiency as a carrier. The fact is that we built twenty-four of those ships. They all functioned beautifully, not one of them was sunk, and all of them are afloat today in July 1970.

Miss Kitchen: It's a wonderful tribute to him. I wonder if he has been accorded the place he should have in naval history.

Admiral Lee: I don't know. He deserves a good share for that job, and for many other jobs that he had. He's now working for the Boeing Company.

He was a man of great ability and foresight, and he applied it in making those ships very workable as aircraft carriers. They were superb ships. Some, twenty-five years later, are still on active duty.

Anyway we found out that these things that he had been fighting for worked really well at Marcus - comparatively few bugs, and with assets that we never knew were there but turned out to be there.

Miss Kitchen: Until you got in combat.

Admiral Lee: Yes. When we came back from the Marcus Island expedition, as I recall, the next thing was the landing on Tarawa.

Miss Kitchen: These first few strikes were, as you spoke, of the nature of a training strike to show or to keep the Japanese off balance and to show them psychologically that we could go that far and have the resilience to come back.

Admiral Lee: That's right, and it was an eye opener to the Japs, too, I think. They were quite impressed.

Miss Kitchen: That would have been in November when you went down to Rabaul.

Admiral Lee: Yes. The aircraft carriers went down to the South Pacific at that time in connection with the campaign against Guadalcanal. We made strikes against the Japanese shipping and shore bases in that area. Rabaul was one of the principal bases of the Japanese. To knock out the ships at Rabaul would be a great asset to us militarily. The loss of their merchant ships was ultimately the thing that hurt Japan the most.

We worked from an anchorage at Epiritu Santu in the New Hebrides. The YORKTOWN and ESSEX sortied from there to make the carrier strikes against the shipping concentrated in Rabaul. Our intelligence wasn't too awfully good in some respects because I don't think we were aware of the fact that most of the Japanese naval air group survivors of the battles of the carriers they had lost earlier in the battle of the Coral Sea were then land-based near Rabaul. They had a whole bunch of naval aircraft down there but with no ships to put them on at the moment, but available to oppose our strikes.

Some strikes had been made before the ESSEX had arrived, but the ESSEX made two strikes which were very successful. In the second strike the Japanese instead of fighting our airplanes made a major attack on the ESSEX. This was our first real taste of battle for the crew of the ship, because the whole air battle was fought very close to the shore and almost over our ship.

The ESSEX was the first ship to arrive out there with any reasonable kind of CIC with radar in it, and this was the first real test of radar in control of aircraft.

By that time I had become exec of the ESSEX (I didn't last as Air Officer very long), and my battle station was in the ESSEX CIC, as the CIC officer. Captain Ofstie was the skipper of the ESSEX. This was one of the earliest uses of an effective CIC in air defense. We were trying to use our new radar, which worked well at long range in the early stages of the battle, but it soon became too much of a melee in which we didn't know whether we were shooting at our own planes or the Japanese planes. But it was very exciting. We saw planes trying to dive on us and hurt us, but nobody actually damaged the ship at all. On the other hand, quite a number of Japanese planes were shot down in sight of us, and some of our own people were shot down. We were very keyed up as you always are in combat. They probably were not hit, but a couple of them that we fired at we found out later were our own people. Some of them landed in the water and went floating by the ship in little rubber boats and we fired at them from the deck of the ship. Some were our own pilots. They were picked up later and saved, but it was just one of the exigencies of war.

This battle gave the ship a great deal of confidence. The actual exchange of aircraft, those lost by the Japanese and those lost by us, were very greatly in our favor, and there was a great deal of damage done by our planes in Rabaul. The whole thing was a good maneuver for us.

We went back from Guadalcanal to support the invasion of Tarawa by making strikes at the enemy bases ashore. These were aimed at their defensive aircraft, and what gun installations we could find before the actual landing was made - softening up the defenses, so to speak. This became sort of a maneuver for us for a lot of the rest of the war, making the fast carrier strikes that took out the Japanese defense before we went in on foot to capture the base. We did this at Tarawa. Rarely in these experiences were we attacked ourselves by enemy aircraft. We were able to stay outside of the range of their aircraft and their defensive aircraft were usually engaged in attacking our aircraft, who were attacking them. The ships, themselves, were maybe a hundred and fifty miles away. So we didn't see much active firing in most of those episodes. The story was told to us by the pilots that came back. I was never allowed to leave the ship, so I never did anything in the air against those installations.

They usually were highly successful as history has shown. We were able to do the things we wanted to do. The only times that we were opposed were usually by Japanese land based bombers of the Betty or Kate or Emily type that came out and attacked us, usually at night. They were uncomfortable for us because you could see them coming on the radar. Our means of shooting them down at night with radar directed guns was not efficient because the planes came in low over the water. We couldn't see the airplanes, all we could see was the radar blip at long range. We were not sufficiently advanced technically to shoot these planes down at night before they could drop their torpedoes. We had carrier damage for that reason from torpedoes from Japanese shore based aircraft, mostly at night.

I can remember spending many unhappy hours in the CIC of the ESSEX watching these blips coming at us, knowing what they were doing, and hoping that our guns would shoot them down, and seeing them turn around on the radar screen, and then knowing that the torpedoes were in the water and on their way to you. Those minutes seemed like years, when you are sitting there waiting to see whether you're going to get hit.

The ESSEX was never hit by a torpedo while I was on it, and that was a long time, but the ships with us were. The new LEXINGTON was hit in our immediate company. And we had torpedoes going by our stern and our bow and even under us sometimes, but they didn't explode. The LEXINGTON was hit right in the stern knocking out her steering, and we had to escort her for quite a long way until she was out of Japanese plane range.

Miss Kitchen: Was this at Tarawa?

Admiral Lee: No, I think that happened off Truk later on.

Miss Kitchen: But when you saw the blips you weren't sure which ship it was going to hit.

Admiral Lee: No, you didn't know. We were always in a formation. There were always at least two carriers, sometimes three carriers, and as many as ten or twelve destroyers in the task force.

Miss Kitchen: To me it would be much worse being inside even though you know what's going on, than to be topside and be able to see something.

Admiral Lee: Well, it's not a happy place to be. It was interesting psychologically to me, even then at the time. It was my first experience of real fear - being in the face of what you thoughtmight be death at any moment, and was interested too in seeing how other people took it. Here you sat around these radar screens and watched these things happen with young seamen who were eighteen or nineteen years old, just off the farm or out of the shoe store, or what have you, and their reactions were for the most part wonderful. Every once in awhile you'd find one that couldn't take it. You could usually see this coming and I found that I could spot when somebody was getting a little hysterical or was about to be hysterical. Not many cases. You could see that some poor kid was getting too emotional. If he got very emotional it would spread, so you had to think of something quick - sending him out to do something right away and get him out. I found that I benefited myself. I was the senior officer in the place, and by looking around carefully to find any evidence of this, I took my own mind off my own problem.

Lots of times I wouldn't like to say things on the microphone to the skipper because you just didn't want the men around you to hear what you were saying. It might be misinterpreted or something or not encouraging, when you didn't want it to be discouraging. Often I would write on a little slip of paper and say, "Run this down to the captain." We were on the deck above the bridge. In those days we were way up in the top in CIC; now you're down at the bottom. I would quickly write a note, which said virtually nothing. This was just to send a message to Captain Ofstie by a runner from CIC, and half the time in those circumstances it was just to get the messenger's mind off his problem.

Miss Kitchen: Did Captain Ofstie understand what you were doing

Admiral Lee: Yes, he knew what I was doing. We had an agreement between us.

Miss Kitchen: It seems to me psychologically it would be a wonderful thing to do.

Admiral Lee: Well, we had a few who lost control of themselves and started weeping, crying, praying, and things like that. Nobody minds people praying, but it's not quite a happy circumstance for men at their battle station.

Miss Kitchen: How many were in the CIC room?

Admiral Lee: In that little CIC, which was primitive by modern standards, there were twelve, fourteen people. I don't want to magnify this. It was a human relations thing which was interesting to me. I found it in other circumstances in other times in the war, too.

Our pattern of most of the ESSEX strikes, of which I was concerned was basically this: listening to the stories of our pilots and how successful they would be, making preparations for sending them off and returning them, taking care of the wounded when they came back wounded, things like that, taking care of airplanes that were damaged, deciding whether to tell them to land in the sea or try to land on the ship.

Miss Kitchen: Was that your responsibility?

Admiral Lee: Yes, and no. The skipper's essentially, but I was the one that made the recommendation. And damaged planes did sometimes land and made a crash on the deck which had to be taken care of, sometimes pushed over the side.

This was the routine which applied to practically all the invasions in so far as the ESSEX was concerned. Attacks by bombers on the ship were relatively infrequent. I don't think I can recall more than five, six, or seven nights that we went through this, but it was always very impressive when we did.

Miss Kitchen: Why were Betty, Kate, and Emily given those names?

Admiral Lee: The Japanese didn't call them that. These were chosen by people in the office of naval intelligence charged with getting out the recognition manuals. They decided on names for various kinds of airplanes or enemy equipments. We have the same thing going on today. We still give our own nicknames to foreign equipments.

Miss Kitchen: Betty then was an intelligence name to identify a type of Japanese plane?

Admiral Lee: Yes. It would be the same as calling it a Phamtom II. The Japanese may have called it the Phamton II, which is the name of one of our airplanes right now, the F-4.

Miss Kitchen: I don't want to leave out the fact that at the Marshalls you were in the strike against Kwajalein in December of '43.

Admiral Lee: Yes, and several others - Eniwetok.

Miss Kitchen: I want to have you describe Truk in 1944.

Admiral Lee: Truk is one of the largest atolls in the world. It's different than most coral atolls in that it has big mountains in the middle of it, quite a good deal of land area, and then a tremendous coral reef all the way around it. It's the largest protected anchorage in the world, one of the largest, and was long known as the headquarters for all the Japanese governmental activities in the southern Pacific. It was considered impregnable partly because the Japanese advertised it as being that way. At least it had that aura in the minds of most of our sailors out there. So when it was learned that we were going to make a raid on Truk, everybody had their fingers crossed. In the ship's paper, the morning after we heard about it, appeared a cartoon, a very graphic picture, a sort of helicopter view of the ESSEX showing the message coming out of the loudspeakers announcing the impending attack on Truk. From almost every port hole and vantage point on deck it showed sailors jumping overboard and starting to swim rather than stay on the ship for the raid.

Miss Kitchen: Remarkable that someone could take it with a sense of humor, isn't it?

Admiral Lee: Oh, there's plenty of that all the time. It was standard. I still have a lot of doggerel poetry written by various people on board making fun of the things that were happening.

As far as I was concerned, I never saw Truk even dimly on the horizon. Our planes attacked it successfully. They sank a number of ships and had very few losses. I recall an anecdote with which I was only slightly associated. A present Vice Admiral of the Navy is Admiral William Martin, now Deputy Commander in Chief, the Atlantic Fleet. He was a pilot on our ship (or one of the ships with us) and was shot down over Truk lagoon and landed in the water there. His plane sank and he was in his life raft in the water inside the reef. The cruiser, BALTIMORE, was with us. The BALTIMORE sent in their small seaplane to pick up Martin. This was done in several other places in the Pacific, and it was quite a risk for the pilot of the seaplane. This little BALTIMORE seaplane came in and spotted Martin in the water and with guns shooting at him from the beach, he landed and Martin was able to climb onto the pontoon. He was awful tired with swimming and the strain he'd been through, and it was hard for him to climb up from the pontoon to the cockpit of the seaplane. He was a commander and the ensign who was flying the plane knew that he was a commander, because he had been told to go rescue Commander Martin. So he went, found him, and did, but Martin was so slow getting up and there were so many bullets going around that the young ensign said, "God damn it, Commander, will you please shake a leg and climb faster -- sir."

Miss Kitchen: And then you went on to the invasion of the Marshall Islands?

Admiral Lee: Yes.

Miss Kitchen: I note that the ESSEX received the Presidential Unit Citation.

Admiral Lee: It's just one of those things for participating in a certain number of operations. Our air groups were always very successful - the real heroism, when there was any, was almost always in the person of the pilots who were sticking their necks out. A lot of them were lost. The crew on board ship, in the big carriers at least, were, except in the big carrier battles in which some of them were badly damaged, relatively out of the picture from bullet problems, bomb problems. At least this was the case in my time in the ESSEX. The ESSEX never received a bullet in her to my recollection, when I was on it. I think we did have a few machine gun bullets in the attacks off Rabaul, but they were practically nothing. The pilots and the air crews bore the brunt of the fighting.

The stress and strain, the long hours at sea, and being exposed to fire as the young pilots were all the time was overcome in some respect by letting the flight surgeon of an air group, or the ship, prescribe for a pilot who has come back from a combat mission, one of these small sample bottles of whiskey which the carriers had a plentiful supply of. They were used by the flight surgeons as a sedative for the nerves of the combat weary pilots. It got to be, on the long watches at sea, that the flight surgeons were importuned to give these bottles of whiskey to people who sometimes didn't need them, but were recounting experiences that indicated they did. Some times they wouldn't drink them right away but would save them and when several of them got quite a number they would have a party in their bunk room somewhere, which wasn't legal and was bad for ship discipline. On other occasions they would use them as gambling stakes in card games. It became a bit of a sticky situation, as to how we could best get this back on the track.

We had a very fine senior doctor on the ESSEX. His name was MacDonald. He had a wonderful personality and was a very good psychologist. After talking our problem over we evolved a program which proved effective. He said, "Let us say that anybody in the crew of the ESSEX could have a miniature bottle of whiskey if his next immediate senior in the line of command, even though he was a seaman first class and had a seaman second class working for him, if the immediate senior would certify that this man had been exposed to a long stint of very hard work in disagreeable conditions, exposed in the wind, or working on something that was difficult and required great physical endurance, that he could prescribe a bottle of whiskey for him merely by taking him down to sick bay where the medical whiskey was kept and writing out a prescription for him and certifying what it was for and then watching him drink it in sick bay."

The last part was the catch, but it worked. We found this solved our problems and produced dividends. The practice was emulated by other ships later on to their benefit. We found that there were many men who deserved these bottles of "medical" whiskey who weren't aviators, and hadn't been exposed to enemy fire but needed a sedative just as badly. When they started to get some which was helpful to them the whole spirit of the thing changed. The aviators didn't mind it, except for a small vocal minority. The abuse of the privilege was given a hundred and eighty degree turn around, and the total quantity consumed was considerably reduced.

1 Lee - 103

Miss Kitchen: It certainly is an example of leadership.

Admiral Lee: I think leadership is finding how to make men work harder to do a better job and to like it.

Miss Kitchen: Did you have occasion to certify the need for alcohol for the aviators?

Admiral Lee: I certainly had the authority to if I wanted to. I was the exec of the ship at the time, but I can't recall that I ever did because I had no person except the heads of departments and a marine orderly working for me directly in that way.

Miss Kitchen: Before we leave the ESSEX, will you tell me the circumstances of how you happened to get married aboard the ESSEX when there were no women aboard?

Admiral Lee: When the ESSEX was being fitted out in Norfolk, I met a very lovely widow of a naval aviator whom I had met before when her husband was a flight student of mine in Pensacola. We were very much attracted to each other and decided to get married, but there wasn't time to do it before I left Norfolk, in proper fashion. Since there were some aspects of not knowing what would happen in the war years, and so forth, we found that we could be married by proxy while I was on the

1 Lee - 104

ESSEX and she was in Norfolk. So we undertook to do that principally for the business of a joint estate, of insurance, and other aspects. She had a small child of her previous marriage. I had to provide a proxy wife on the ESSEX for me, and she had to provide a proxy husband for herself, who turned out to be her uncle. We were married under a "ceremony" that is issued I think by the Department of Justice. The proxy on my end of the line was the air group commander, Commander Charles D. Griffin. He became my legal wife by proxy for the remainder of the time until I was actually married later on in San Francisco with my wife.

Miss Kitchen: Did he behave properly after that?

Admiral Lee: Not as a wife, no. He was a very good air group commander, though.

Miss Kitchen: Describe the circumstances. Where were you?

Admiral Lee: We were at sea on the ESSEX, and this was arranged by radio message. We could get the word by radio that it was authorized. It had been arranged by mail before hand, and then it was authorized by the judge in Norfolk.

Miss Kitchen: Who performed it? Was it an actual ceremony?

1 Lee - 105

Admiral Lee: Admiral Ofstie performed it for me and Commander Griffin.

Miss Kitchen: Did he say the regular words?

Admiral Lee: No, it wasn't a ceremony of that kind. Commander Griffin spoke the words saying I was present at the occasion, certified that this woman was the one that I wanted to be married to, and he verified the fact that he knew these facts to be true. But in the law he is actually the proxy wife until the marriage is actually made.

Miss Kitchen: Did she go through the same type of ceremony?

Admiral Lee: Yes. It has to be authorized by a judge saying it is desirable for these people to be married and impossible for them to be married under the circumstances, and these people who are familiar with these people knew this fact. Commander Griffin knew the girl in Norfolk. We had been house guests in his home in Norfolk. Because it was all known in this way it was easily arranged.

Miss Kitchen: So then you were actually legally married, although by proxy?

Admiral Lee: From all the points of view of civil law we were married. Every legal aspect pertaining to actual marriage from the point of view of the law was valid from that point forward.

Miss Kitchen: Would it have been necessary for you ever to have had a civil marriage if you hadn't wanted to?

Admiral Lee: I believe it would have been, but I don't recall exactly if it would or not.

Miss Kitchen: Why did you go from the ESSEX to your next job?

Admiral Lee: I had been on the ESSEX for about eighteen months and the Navy was expanding still. They formed a new carrier division, commander and his staff, to take charge of one of the carrier task groups operations in the Pacific. This new staff was to be under the command of Admiral Frank Wagner, and I was ordered as his chief of staff. Our job was to get the staff together, get it trained, get it organized, and then go to work as a carrier task group commander.

Miss Kitchen: Where were you?

Admiral Lee: In Pearl Harbor. We started in Pearl Harbor and actually, to put this in perspective, we never got a command. One thing and another changed very fast and the whole staff was disbanded because other arrangements were being made. I've forgotten the duration of our period but it covered only about two or three months probably. The first thing was to get the staff together and organized and you had to take what people they sent you. The people that did come were very competant people. I will not forget one of them who became the flag secretary. I thought I could handle him all right because I had been a flag secretary a couple of times before, and even though he was just a war time navy volunteer I could steer him in doing his job. Well, he turned out to be Douglas Dillon, the head of Dillon and Company in Wall Street, and a brilliant man who served in government in high posts in the State Department and Defense Department in later years. He was one of those lucky individuals with a photographic memory; he could remember every fact and face no matter where he saw it or where he read it. Such a man is a gem in anybody's organization because he always knew the pertinent facts and figures. He was a delightful person, extremely efficient and very quiet, and a nice person to have.

We were sent to the carrier WASP and went out and trained an air group on the carrier WASP just as a part of the shakedown training of a new air group with a new admiral. When we, the staff, weren't training a new air group we visited on various other ships and staffs to get an idea of how they were working before we took our final assignment.

One phase of this might be of interest. It was another question of leadership, something I have always had a great deal of interest in. We had two or three cases of battle weary pilots. They came back from combat and were on their second tour in another air group to go out and work again. Some were emotionally unstable and shouldn't have been sent back to combat. It so happened that in our training air group quite a number of these pilots were assigned to see if it was all right to send them back to combat or not, to let us look them over a little bit before we did so. It was an interesting study in psychology. We never solved it. It's an insoluble problem. You don't know what the man really wants and he won't tell you, and he is not going to admit that he's afraid to go back, or would give his left arm if he wasn't sent back. He deosn't want to be called a coward. You don't want to make him a coward if he isn't one. You have to decide whether this man with his valuable experience and training, who could be so valuable, should be sent to a combat job or back to shore duty with no opprobrium attached to his record.

It was my lot to decide quite a number of these cases. Admiral Wagner is now deceased. He and I disagreed in many of these cases - we just didn't see things eye to eye, so we got into some arguments about it. I felt that we should often confront the person with, "What do you really want to do?" There was an aura of not doing it this way and some psychologists had counseled against it. I said, "Just let me talk to the fellow and I think between the two of us I can decide. I would tell this guy that we're not going to send him back because he's not in a fit mental condition to go but we're not going to put anything derogatory about him other than combat fatigue." Admiral Wagner disagreed with that. He said, "Okay, you can talk to them all you please but if you send them back to the States, and they say they want to go back, then that fact's got to go in the record."

So we had arguments about it. I had officers who did go back and who came and served with me later and I knew their record, and they knew I knew their record, but nobody else knew their record. It's something I lived with and was never sure about. I don't know why I tell you about it now. It just came to mind in connection with my duties on the WASP when we really didn't have very much to do in the short period I was there.

Miss Kitchen: Would they say to you, "I don't think that it's wise to send me into combat again." Or would you tell by their manner, or was it an aura that gave you a clue?

Admiral Lee: I wasn't the only one that talked to them. There were two or three people who talked to them, but they quickly sensed why we were talking to them even if we didn't come out boldly and say so. Many of them were quite clear cut cases that worked out all right, but there were many you wanted to save face for themselves, and you didn't know how to do it. You couldn't play God and you really were put into a position of playing God. But it worked out.

Miss Kitchen: Did you later have any feelings of making decisions that you found had been wrong, or were you ever able to follow up in the individual cases to that extent?

Admiral Lee: I knew some of the people later on. We knew of our previous relationships and I never mentioned them again and neither did they. We both did that by mutual understanding, I think. Neither of us brought it up. I think it was the best way. I don't know that we had any particular problem or whether I found out I was right in one case and wrong in another, I don't know. We would have the problem of finding out.

For instance, a pilot might be a scheduling officer, and he would never schedule himself to go out on a combat mission. His plane would always have something wrong with it, or he had a headache, or something like that. Then his skipper would notice this and say, "I'm not sure this fellow ought to do this." If you talked to the guy he would swear up and down that he never did this, but statistically it was obvious that he did. So you had to tell him he was going back, and then he would fight it and say, "No, I don't want to. I want to stay here in the squadron."

Miss Kitchen: But you had the responsibility not only of saving his life but other men's lives for which he was responsible.

Admiral Lee: It was an interesting interlude.

Miss Kitchen: You said that staff never was assigned but was broken up and went to different jobs?

Admiral Lee: That was the case but while we were in this sort of interlude status as a "makee-learn" job for us, we went over and visited other staffs. It was for that reason that I was on the BUNKER HILL with Admiral Mitscher in the battles for the Philippine Sea. I happened to be temporarily assigned to his staff when that battle occurred and I went through the three or four days of it with him and his staff officers. It was quite an experience because the BUNKER HILL was under fire and the times were very tense, and big decisions had to be made. Also the ship was damaged. It was the big decision when Admiral Mitscher decided to light up the whole fleet at night to let the returning pilots have a better chance to find us. We had some Japanese airplanes that got mixed up with our airplanes coming back. One of them made about four passes trying to land on the BUNKER HILL at night. We wouldn't let him because we were afraid his hook wouldn't fit our arresting wires and would do a lot of damage on deck, so we kept shooting at him with very pistols to ward him off. He finally gave up the attempt and went off and was lost at sea in all probability.

A big decision came on the issue as to how far to send our air groups with the knowledge that some of them probably wouldn't have the gasoline endurance to get back to the ship in any circumstances. Some of them would come back after dark and, at that stage of the war, not all the pilots were night qualified. Many of them would have to make their first landing at night in these circumstances, and the ships would be darkened which was then the absolute doctrine. Admiral Mitscher made the decision to turn on every light in the fleet and put the search lights up because many of them were having a hard time finding their way back. Many of them did not make it. Quite a number were able to get back and land in the water alongside ships and were picked up and saved. But a big percentage of them did return and landed safely if they had enough gasoline to do it.

Miss Kitchen: What was your job on the BUNKER HILL?

Admiral Lee: I was nothing. I was really only an observer. I was working with the operations officer and the chief of staff, who was a Captain Hedding, and Admiral Mitscher. But really just as an observer - no responsibilities.

Miss Kitchen: It was an important battle and I don't want you to leave out any item that you can recall of Admiral Mitscher or the operation.

Admiral Lee: The big tactical decision was how far to send these people to get ships that we thought were going to threaten our ships. Admiral Spruance was the head decision maker and he was the one that decided not to go any farther. This became one of the critical decisions of the whole war, and has been much argued. Some people say it was unsound but I think history has shown that Admiral Spruance was probably one of the finest minds that we had at work in the Pacific Fleet, and that his decisions were essentially sound at Midway, and elsewhere, including the battle of the Philippine Sea. We did make some effort to stretch things and hit the ships. They were mostly tankers we wanted to get. If we could get the tankers, we were safe because the Japanese combat ships wouldn't have the fuel which the tankers were taking to them, and they needed it badly.

It was a melodramatic night with all these planes coming back and all the ships with big search lights trained up in the air. It was sort of cloudy and messy weather, with heavy seas. Planes were landing in the water, destroyers coming and trying to pick them up and not always able to pick them out of the water right in the sight of search lights. It was grim. We had a couple of people who crashed on the deck which complicated things because then you had to stop landing so you could clear the wreckage. But I was simply an observer.

Miss Kitchen: But you saw an important part of history.

Admiral Lee: It was important to me, yes. But I took no part in making any decisions or in doing anything helpful other than handling somebody a pencil or a handkerchief or whatever they wanted.

And that's the end of my first duty in Carrier Division Five. About ten years later I joined Carrier Division Five again as the Admiral.

I was ordered next to the command of the carrier MANILA BAY, an escort or "jeep" carrier. The MANILA BAY had just had some minor repairs done to her when I took over, which was in Pearl Harbor. I was surprised to find that I was to take command of a ship and that the skipper had left before I even got there. This was rather unusual to me in my previous experience in the Navy, but I soon found it was routine in war time.

I might say a word or two about the Kaiser jeep carriers. The United States built some hundred and thirteen of these carriers for the United States in World War II and quite a number (I've forgotten how many) for Britain, and a couple of other countries. They were built on production lines on the West Coast and the majority of the workers who constructed them were women. They tell many fantastic stories about the rapid building of the ships. One of them was that when a lady was christening one, missed her swing with the champagne bottle, and was told that, "Stand here for another forty minutes, and we'll have another one ready." This was apocryphal but not too far from being representative of the actualities of building those ships.

For this reason we were constantly finding, as the operators of the ships, that they had some peculiar characteristics, and sometimes rather make-shift arrangements in places that broke down when least expected or when least desired. Their main engines were called Uni-flow engines. These were unique to a small class of ore carrying ships on the Great Lakes. Inasmuch as they had a plant there that was manufacturing these engines, and they had to use all the plant capacity they could in war time, it was decreed that they would keep on making Uni-flow engines up there and would put them in all the jeep carriers. They weren't too bad but they were unique in design and no ordinary machinist or engineman - the products of our war time technical schools - had any knowledge of how to operate them. So they were always troublesome. We found many engineering difficulties which sprung from the non-standard design and the lack of spare parts. Another characteristic which was disturbing was that the gauge of the metal used in constructing the ships was very light. They crinkled and crackled like a tin can when the ship rolled or pitched and yawed in heavy seas. To go through a typhoon in one of them, which I did, was an experience. The noise of the ship just creaking and cracking coupled with very heavy rolling was quite unnerving to people who hadn't been to sea before as well as to many who had been, such as I.

In the battles for Leyte Gulf, which I will mention in a few minutes, several of the eight inch shells of the Japanese cruisers attacking the small aircraft carriers went in one side of the carrier, through the hangar deck, out the other side, and on off into the water. They exploded when they finally hit the water because the water was harder than the sides of the ship. Of course the shells were fused to go off only on a heavy impact. They were armor piercing shells designed by the Japanese to hit armored war ships, and they weren't even slightly embarrassed by going through both sides of our jeep carriers. We were embarrassed, but happy.

We proceeded directly from Pearl Harbor in MANILA BAY to a placed called Manus, in the New Hebrides where the forces were being assembled to make the amphibious landings on Leyte Island in the Philippines, the first step by MacArthur in the invasion of the Philippines. Manus was a way out of the way spot. We stayed there for several weeks as they assembled the forces there. It is in the New Hebrides which few people had ever gone to before and nobody had worried about much. The natives were Negroid, distinctive, interesting, and very primitive. There was nothing to do but welter and swelter in the heat for quite a while.

While at anchor in Manus an ammunition ship, the MT.HOOD, was anchored fairly near us loaded full of ammunition. While dispensing some of it to the ships in the harbor, it blew up - one of the major disasters of the war. It damaged quite a number of ships besides itself and the one that was alongside, both of which practically disappeared - only fragments were found. The explosion was a whopper and the MANILA BAY was anchored probably about three or four thousand yards away. I was in the wardroom with some other officers when it happened. We all thought at first that someone had fired our one five inch gun, which sits on the stern as the main battery of a jeep carrier. When it is fired, it is quite apparent that something big has happened: the whole ship jumps. So when it jumped from the explosion we all thought somebody had fired our gun. We knew it shouldn't have been fired and we were fran

We all started rushing for the stern to see what was happening. When we got on deck, we found people looking at the mushroom cloud, just like the atomic cloud, that went up from the explosion.

Before proceeding to the invasion of the Philippines, let me take a moment to set the scene, so to speak. The southern part of the Philippines consists of quite a number of islands which enclose the Sulu Sea. There are only two exits to this sea into the Pacific — one is called the San Bernardino Strait, which is to the northward near Luzon (the big island), and the other one is the Surigao Strait between Leyte and Mindanao at the southern end of the Philippines. The plan of the Americans was to land on the Pacific side of Leyte Island, which is central, and between the two straits. If this were successful we were to proceed northward, playing it somewhat by ear, but taking our forces through the Sulu Sea around to the China Sea side of the Philippines, going up past Manila and making a second invasion about ninety miles north of Manila at Lingayen Gulf. The troops at Lingayen would then fight their way south and recapture Manila.

The Japanese had been in occupation of the Philippines for quite a time. They had many air fields ashore there. They were just starting the use of the Kamikaze pilots. They had trained them for some time. We had heard vague reports of their doing something like that. We thought it might happen but we didn't know really if it was true (at least I didn't) and suspected that it wasn't because it was a hard thing to imagine that anyone could train a sizeable force for such a purpose. Anyway the Japanese occupied many small landing fields suitable for their airplanes throughout the Philippines.

Their major forces, knowing we were coming in to the Philippines, were concentrated in northern Borneo and the southern Philippines under Admiral Kurita. He had the job of preventing our invasion. He elected to do this by sending part of his force northward through the San Bernardino Straits, and part southward through the Surigao Strait to attack our ships off Leyte. The part that went out from San Bernardino was to join up with some reinforcements that were coming from Japan, which were the rag-tag of what was left that could do anything in the Japanese home waters, and included two large ships which had been modified into semi-aircraft carriers and which our intelligence classified as aircraft carriers. They really weren't carriers and were incapable of acting like one in a meaningful way. These forces were coming south, and Kurita's northern forces would join with them.

This would be a major force which we had to oppose, and the people coming through the Surigao Straits would have to be opposed locally just off the island of Leyte. There were some eighteen jeep carriers in the forces assigned to General MacArthur for this campaign. They were divided into three carrier groups. In the support of the first landings in Leyte, our ships were there giving the close air support to the troops. There was nothing to attack ashore because the Japanese didn't know where we were going to land. They couldn't put any permanent forces ashore in the spot to oppose us really. The minute we got there and until we got a few air strips going, we had to supply all of the close air support for all the landings in Leyte and Samar.

Kurita's forces were somewhat depleted on their way out by submarine attacks in the Sulu Sea, and they had poor communications with their homeland so all Kurita knew was that he had to join up with this other force and do the best he could to sink as many ships that were engaged in landing troops in the Philippines. The first phases of this battle were almost routine for us. We just sent off planes engaged in close air support for the Army troops that were going ashore in routine unopposed amphibious landings. It wasn't until we got positive word of the approach of these Japanese forces that we knew that we were in for a major battle. At least I, as the skipper of one of the jeep carriers, had my first knowledge of it then.

On the day we were attacked we were in three circular carrier formations in a north south line with about seven or eight miles, maybe ten miles, I would say between groups. We could just see the group to the north of us and we could not even see the third group which was even farther north over the horizon. We were the southern-most group, and my group was the one that was the least attacked by the forces which actually turned out to be those under Kurita coming out of the Bernardino Straits. He came out with the super battleship MUSASHI which was probably one of the most lethal fighting ships ever made. It was a super battleship, the sister ship of the YAMATO. There were only two of them and they were heavily armed and armored as any ship ever built. Kurita had a couple of heavy cruisers which were the first to come through the San Bernardino Straits and headed south towards us. The first, almost, that we knew of them was only an hour or two before they started shooting at our jeep carriers, who were more or less sitting ducks. The Japanese ships had speeds of up to twenty-seven or thirty knots. I don't know exactly what their speed was. Our maximum with our Uni-flow engines flowing as fast as they could was a hopefully eighteen knots. And when you went that fast for long you had the fear that something would break and you'd have to slow up.

As soon as we knew of their presence every effort of the jeep carriers was to damage or sink these ships with our aircraft, and also to put as much distance as we could between the attacking ships and ourselves which meant that we turned to a southeasterly heading and went as fast as we could. We did all our launching and landing airplanes after that regardless of the direction of the wind by simply going as fast as we could away from the Japanese. This was not good, but I can't recall any take-off or landing accidents that were caused by insufficient wind across the deck. Everybody knew it was for keeps; they were on their toes to do the best they could and they did.

We, of course, started sending off groups of airplanes in reasonable tactical groups - everybody in good shape and all set. But after the first attacks were made and we lost a good many of the planes, there was much confusion as they came back. The actual procedure, as I saw it from my bridge, was that it was every pilot for himself - he landed on any carrier he could find, he got some more ammunition, and went back to deliver it against the attacking ships, then came back and tried to find a landing deck open to land and be loaded again. This went on for quite a number of hours.

There were shells fired from heavy cruisers into our carrier formation. None of them hit the MANILA BAY, although the splashes fell between our escort destroyers and us. We could just barely see the top of the cruiser's mast that was firing at us over the horizon. It was disconcerting because they kept shooting for some time, and you didn't know when the next one was going to hit you. As the time went on, it became apparent that unless we could sink the ships, we were all going to be sunk by the guns of the ships because there was nobody else around that could help us. So it was a rather unhappy passage of time with nothing seeming to change much. We obviously weren't sinking these cruisers and the big battleship MUSASHI. Time was on their side.

I might add that the fighter airplanes that were embarked in these little jeep carriers were the little F4F's. They were good small fighter planes, but had practically no capability against anything like a fighting war ship. The torpedo planes were the old Martin and Grummun TBM's, the "turkeys" they were called. They could carry a torpedo and bombs. The most useful weapon they could carry was a torpedo, against these ships. It was Torpedo Squadron Eight at Midway which was launched against the Japanese ships, and the whole squadron went in and none came back. They were all shot down because a torpedo depends on the plane making a straight run for awhile right within the range of the batteries of the target ships. So we lost a lot of our torpedo planes. However, we ran out of torpedoes before we lost all the planes that could shoot them.

It was my unhappy experience (I remember this more vividly, perhaps, than almost anything in the war) to have a torpedo plane land on my ship, who wasn't one of our air group. He had made two attacks on the MUSASHI with his torpedoes from his own ship. The doctrine was - you load him up again and sent him off. He was pretty shaken up because he had watched his pals get shot down and he had made two passes and done his best. We had just one torpedo left. I had to tell this young man that he had to take that torpedo and go back and make a third try. I wasn't too sure that I was doing the right thing, but we didn't have any other pilot on board. Ours were all flying. So we loaded him up and I gave him a fight talk on the bridge and patted him on the back and said, "Go out and do your best." He did make a third run and he landed on another ship and he survived, I heard later. I was quite moved by this at the time. I thought after I had sent him off that if I'd scouted around I probably could have found a volunteer who was good enough at flying that kind of airplane who could have taken off and done it. And I hadn't done that - after thoughts do you no good. But it worked out all right as far as his making his effort and doing the best he could, and we'd done the best we could.

None of the Japanese ships were sunk and some of our ships had, and we were on our way to being wiped out fairly soon unless something happened, and there was nothing in prospect that could happen that would help us much.

Then the completely unforseen did happen. Admiral Kurita, for reasons completely unknown to any of us at that time and for many months afterwards, suddenly turned around and went off to the north. He could have easily, with the ammunition available to him and the circumstances at the time, sunk all eighteen carriers, probably. Maybe if we had scattered he couldn't have found all of us, but he could have sunk quite a number. But he did turn back, and subsequently after the war he said that he had had a complete lack of communications, he got garbled messages, and thought he was supposed to join and reenforce the ships that were coming down from the north. It was a misunderstanding. I don't think the Japanese ever forgave him, but we were glad that he did what he did.

That was really about the extent of our participation in the battle. I was awfully happy to see the way all our ships performed. We didn't have any basic troubles. All the pilots did their utmost and there was nothing that I knew of that didn't reflect the greatest credit under the most difficult circumstances on the part of all hands. It made me feel good.

Our group commander was Admiral Felix Stump. He was quite a colorful character and still is, a very fine man and good friend of mine. I've worked with him and for him many times. He's nothing if not vocal. He spent all of this long period of the battle with his microphone in his hand talking to all us skippers on his six carriers, giving us all kinds of encouragement, sort of like the football coach running up and down the sidelines shouting signals to the players on the field. Really he didn't give us any tactical order during the whole thing, except to say what the basic course would be and go as fast as we could, and we did that the whole time. Since some of the ships were able to go a little faster than the others we got strung out in a long line for awhile, and I think Admiral Stump got worried for fear that his short range radio words of advice weren't going to reach all his skippers and that was the only thing that phased him. But that was surmise on my part.

Miss Kitchen: I'm sure that the leadership that you gave to your men was as helpful to them as his advice was to you, and one of the reasons that you received the Navy Cross for this action.

Admiral Lee: In such circumstances I think the Navy, rightly so in many ways but mistakenly in others, finds it difficult to reward everybody according to his performance and the principal commanders are given awards in the name of the performance of the ship as a whole. It can happen that the commander might have been something of a dud, but had wonderful people working for him. One of the things in a situation like that is that most of the crew on an aircraft carrier, ninety percent of them I would say, are down below. They can't see anything and they don't know what's happened and they don't know what's going on very much.

We had, early in the game, established a battle watch station for our supply officer who sat up on the bridge; he was the EMCEE for the operation. He talked over our loudspeakers to all the crew down below, telling them what was happening. He didn't have any words of good advice or tell them to do this or that unless he was told to tell them (if that came, his mike was cut off and mine or somebody else's was used). He had the job of trying to paint the picture to the poor fellows slaving down below to keep the ship going, get the ammunition coming up, and doing all the hundreds of other needed things. This was used in many ships. We started it in the ESSEX, but only after we had been operating for some time, and were very pleased with it. A lot depends on the personality of that guy on the microphone. We were fortunate in MANILA BAY in having a young lieutenant, our supply officer, who was a young politician from San Francisco. His father was the Mayor of San Francisco. He had a good nack of choosing topics to talk about and a good voice. He phrased things to encourage but still tell the truth, and had a wonderful sense of humor. I don't think I ever recommended him for an award - but, looking back, I sure should have.

Miss Kitchen: I'm sure he was invaluable.

Admiral Lee: He was, and very much so in our next engagement at Lingayen Gulf.

We were able to recoup quickly from the attacks of the Japanese ships, losing only two of our jeep carriers, I think. The ships coming through Surigao Strait had been completely destroyed almost by our own opposing battleships, so they posed no further threat to us, for which we were very happy. We were aware of the fact that a Japanese force was expected from the north. We knew it was supposed to have Japanese carriers and that it was a threat to our forces. I believe we were aware that Admiral Halsey had gone to oppose those forces. I personally was not aware, or have no recollection of that fact that he had, in going north uncapped or unwatched the exits from San Bernardino Strait, thus permitting the Japanese ships which attacked us to come out unopposed. We couldn't have done anything about it at the time if we had known it, but it was only in the aftermath when all these things were straightened out as to what had happened to whom that we became aware that the ships had come through unopposed.

Miss Kitchen: I think you said that when you knew he had gone north against the aircraft carriers you were glad he had done it, at the time.

Admiral Lee: We certainly were, because they were one of the principal threats to us.

As I look back, when I first took command of the MANILA BAY, I was surprised to see the comparative greenness of our crew. On the big ESSEX carriers we had a pretty good sprinkling of talent. Almost a majority, I think, of the ship's officers on the ESSEX when it was commissioned were Naval Academy graduates. When I got to the MANILA BAY I found that there was only one other officer on the ship who had gone to the Naval Academy and MANILA BAY was the first big ship that at least seventy or eighty percent of the crew had ever been on in their lives. Most of them were from the middle west. They'd gotten a good basic training and all did a good job, but they didn't have the sense of discipline and spit and polish which I had been accustomed to in all my previous years in the Navy. This was a little hard to get used to to begin with, but I certainly had no lack of confidence after I had been aboard for a little while. Everything was going to go all right, and I kept telling myself the Japanese probably had it worse.

We had some very fine men on the MANILA BAY. I don't remember many of their names now but I do remember the fine performances of many of them. Our chief engineer was a man in his late fifties who had been a chief engineer in merchant ships all his life but he'd never seen a uni-flow engine and thought they were terrible and should never have been built. Our doctor had almost given up being a doctor because he had found a more lucrative profession in running a jazz band, so he was useful in promoting musical talent on board ship - he was the leader of our Jazz Band. One of our junior ordinance officers was a young man by the name of Paul Ignatius, who in the sixties served as the Secretary of the Navy.

After our troops were firmly established in the central Philippines, the escort carriers were returned to the harbor of Manus in the New Hebrides to reorganize and get rested for the next step in the invasion. This was to go through the Sulu Sea, south of the island of Mindoro, and on to land at Lingayen for the attack on Manila. Mindoro is just south of the island of Luzon and was heavily defended by the Japanese. They had a lot of air fields on it; it was one of their princip air field bases.

Our passage through the Sulu Sea was pretty hairy because it was our first experience with kamikazes. We were all very jittery. Some of the ships in our vicinity were attacked and one or two of them sunk, as I recall. They seemed to be attacking ships like cruisers and destroyers and tankers, which were good targets for them rather than the carriers at this time, which was a happy situation as far as we were concerned. We were on a constant alert for any Japanese air raid alarm, so to speak, and every time anybody thought he saw a speck on a radar screen, everybody had to rush to general quarters. We wore ourselves out, almost, being ready for things that we really couldn't do much about. MANILA BAY was not attacked by kamikazes in the Sulu Sea, although ships in our formation were attacked. Some were damaged but none sunk.

However, as we approached Lingayen, after we passed Manila on the way north, the kamikaze attacks became more frequent on our ships, and they were attacking the jeep carriers particularly and successfully. The ship next to us in our formation was the carrier OMMANEY BAY, and it was hit by two kamikazes. She was close to us and we didn't know whether they were aiming at us or the OMMANEY BAY early in the attack, but they hit her and sank her. She sank with a large loss of life. Many people were left, however, swimming in the water and in the subsequent rescue operations we brought aboard the MANILA BAY, I think, about a hundred and fifty or seventy-five people from the crew of the OMMANEY BAY.

Miss Kitchen: How did they get aboard?

Admiral Lee: We put down boats and picked them up. Other ships were doing the same thing. They were all trying to rescue all the people we could find.

Miss Kitchen: They didn't have to climb up those rope ladders?

Admiral Lee: The ones we were bringing back in boats had to climb up a rope ladder from the boat into the ship. Some of them were wounded and burned, and we had to put them in stretchers and hoist them up. After that rescue operation was over, we had another twenty-four hours or thirty-six hours of steaming to get to the site of the landing at Lingayen. I got together all of the principal people we had rescued who had any positions of responsibility or capability of observation in key spots in the OMMANEY BAY and asked them to tell me all they knew about what had happened. I think it was the Hangar Deck Officer who told me that they wouldn't have been so severly damaged if they hadn't had a terrible holocaust — the whole hangar deck caught on fire almost simultaneously because every plane in it was filled with gasoline and armed with bombs to go. The hangar virtually exploded in flame and damaged the ship so much it sank pretty quickly. The Hangar Deck Officer was fortunately blown off clear and survived. I said, "Didn't they sound the sprinkler alarm?" He said, "It happened so quickly that we couldn't do it." I said, "If you had had the sprinklers going when it hit, do you think it would work?" He said, "Yes, it would help."

So I got my principal officers together and we concocted a system that if I felt we were about to be hit, almost certainly, I would punch a button that said instantly turn on all the sprinklers in the hangar. Then if they missed we would turn them off and we would have done a lot of damage to planes and things, but it might have been better than losing the ship. So we had this system going.

The next day our formation was attacked several times and another ship was sunk. Two or three kamikazes attacked us specifically. They came across the water, close to the surface of the water. They were small planes, Val's I think they were, and had quite small bombs. They were only about twenty-five or thirty feet off the water. They came out of the late afternoon sun, and we didn't get them in our optical sight, although they had them on radar, for quite a little time. Many ships were shooting guns at them but none of these three was hit. Others were shot down, however. The tactic which most of the kamikaze pilots seemed to be using in that area at that time was to come in low, get under the radar, and then when they were about three hundred, or four hundred, yards from the ship, they would zoom up in a large arcing maneuver which would take them up to about three hundred feet and then come down in an almost vertical dive on the ship. These three planes did this and they all aimed themselves at the MANILA BAY. As they came down in the vertical part of their dives, they fired their machine guns at us too, and they apparently were firing at our bridge - at least the one that hit us was. Only one of the three hit us squarely and he did a great deal of damage. The second one almost missed. He hit the side of the walkway nets and some of the radio antenna boom sticking out from the stern, and we had a little bit of damage there. He went into the water right alongside the ship and exploded damaging the hull a little bit aft, but not seriously. The other, although he made a beautiful big zooming dive, missed us by about fifty or a hundred feet, and didn't do any damage to us at all.

The one that hit actually crashed into the flight deck just at the base of the flight deck island structure. He went right on through that deck and into the next compartment which was a part of our CIC and radar control rooms, and then on into the hangar deck. Part of him went into the hangar deck and part of him stayed on the deck above in the CIC. When he started on this loop down, he started firing machine gun bullets. The two people standing on each side of me were hit by machine gun bullets, although neither of them fatally, but each of them were hit by machine gun bullets that went through their shoulders and upper chests. I wasn't hit. I knew we were going to be hit so I punched the button, and they turned on the sprinkler system in the hangar which is, undoubtedly, what saved the ship because a big fire started, but it was fairly quickly put under control and stopped. If it hadn't been for the loss of the OMMANEY BAY, and the chance to talk to her survivors, we wouldn't have done that.

When the plane exploded, his bombs, himself, and everything exploded right underneath us on the bridge. I had to go by eye witness accounts later on, but all of us on the little top bridge of the ship were thrown up into the air. We were well off the deck. I think I went about four or five feet off in the air. I landed more or less on all fours, on my feet and my hands in a crouching position as I came down on the deck. On the flight deck about twenty feet below me was what we call an airplane tow bar - it's a long steel bar with little wheels on it that is hitched to an airplane, and the forward part has a hook that attaches to a tractor that pulls the airplane around the deck. Those two bars are about fifteen or twenty feet long and about four or five inches in diameter, and they aren't light and feathery. They're made of steel pipe. This thing had gone way up in the air, and it came down partly on top of me, so I was hurt on my back. It bothered me for some time, but it wasn't really a wound or anything. Also the flash from the explosion took almost all the hair and eyebrows and eyelashes, and burned the exposed skin of almost everyone on the bridge. We had our helmets and flash masks on, but there were exposed places which were burned. Just a very severe sunburn is all it was - a terrific sunburn.

I tell you all this to explain a ceremony held a few days later when we were passing out all the Purple Heart medals for the wounded. I think there were about eighteen killed and about seventy wounded by this particular explosion. Anyway we passed out a large number of Purple Hearts. Everybody kept asking me why I didn't get a Purple Heart. I didn't get one because the qualifications for getting a Purple Heart stated you had to be wounded, and in order to be wounded you had to have your skin punctured. My back was sore and black and blue for weeks, but my skin hadn't been punctured anywhere, so I was ineligible for the Purple Heart, while some people with little tiny scratches got Purple Hearts because that was the letter of the law.

All of the electric wires for ship control of these little jeep carriers were in a shaft that came from the power sources down below and through a big tube that went to the bridge in the island structure. They also went into a secondary battle control station which most war ships have which is an alternate command post in case the bridge is wiped out. In the case of the jeep carriers, this alternate is back on the stern. When the bomb went off it severed every wire to the bridge and when the other plane hit at the stern it damaged most of the communications back there. The effect was that nobody inside the ship could talk to anybody on the bridge, where almost all the control personnel were, and nobody could talk to the executive officer who was back at the stern. From that moment on we had to run everything by messenger around the ship to take whatever messages were necessary to fight fire and so forth. This was a terrific handicap. Also we had no radio with which we could talk with anybody else.

They got the fire out fairly soon and we repaired the hole in the flight deck, which wasn't in the middle of the flight deck but on one side of it. The essential parts of the ship were virtually undamaged from most points of view, so for the rest of the engagement at Lingayen we were able to operate our airplanes although with crude and makeshift arrangements. We were very proud of the fact that we could and did.

Oddly enough, we found that one thing that had been damaged and was most dangerous to our aircraft operations subsequently was that the flight deck had gotten sort of a bubble in it due to the explosion in the hangar below. It made a slight mound - it couldn't have been more than six inches high - in the forward part of the flight deck. When our little planes took off and rolled over this mound, the attitude of the plane was changed as it went over it, destroying part of the lift, and slowing the speed that the planes should have had when they got to the bow. You almost always flew the planes off the ship, never catapulted them. So we found that planes that we thought were going to go sailing off into the wild blue younder were falling over the bow and just barely staying above the water for about a hundred and fifty yards before they could get real good flying speed. We had to take out some of the load to compensate after we almost lost two or three planes. I regret to say that I, as the skipper, was poo-pooing this saying, "It's ridiculous. That couldn't be the cause of that little thing. It's just poor pilot technique. Try harder next time." But they were right and I was wrong, and we did remedy it later on.

We establihsed communications with the other ships by using the radio in one or our airplanes on the deck to talk to the Task Group Commander. We only had one low-powered circuit, and we had to operate with that one circuit all the way. We did contribute air support until the end of the landing operations at Lingayen, and when these were completed we came out with the other carriers, and all went back together as far as Leyte.

I was awfully proud with all that went on in the ship. Most of the people down below can't know exactly what is happening, but can know that plenty awful things are happening. Some of the ship was in darkness because light cables had been cut , although in many places they weren't and we did have electric lights in lots of places. We were soon able to start re-rigging and making repairs. But in all of those very trying circumstances with most of the ship in uncertainty as to whether or not we were going to sink like the OMMANEY BAY had, we didn't have one case that I ever found of anybody leaving his station, trying to come up topside, stopping doing what he was supposed to do. This I think was in part due to the officer whom I mentioned a little while ago, the supply officer, Lieutenant Lapham, who kept telling everybody what was happening. He wasn't able to for awhile, but he went down and rigged a temporary cable to the loudspeaker system of the ship, and we were soon able to get his microphone going. He started from that moment telling people belowdecks what had happened and what was happening in a most encouraging way. I went down and talked on that circuit a little while myself, but most of the time it was just this one young officer who was the big factor in keeping up morale and acting as a pumper full of confidence.

Miss Kitchen: Do you know what you said to the crew?

Admiral Lee: No, just encouragement. I do remember the first message we were able to send to Admiral Stump, our boss. Our code name for the ship was "Circus," the code nickname for the voice radio circuit, and our message said, "Circus performance interrupted for awhile. Have two rings operating, expect to have third ring operating soon."

Miss Kitchen: It seems to me that you would have been in extreme pain.

Admiral Lee: Well, I was but you don't think about that. I really didn't start to hurt until about a day afterwards.

Most of my back was black and blue but no skin puncture. Only a few people on the actual bridge platform were killed and those were from machine gun bullets.

During our trip back through the Sulu Sea there were still an awful lot of Japanese airplanes including kamikazes around, and it was a painful trip for us in the MANILA BAY. We had no radar of any kind, and we'd become very dependent on radar to be aware of enemy attacks. We hadn't any good radio that was really dependable. We still had our little airplane radio to use to talk and listen to, but this was a crude rig and not the same at all as having your regular radio communication equipment.

We were put in the rear part of the circular formation which the Task Group cruised in. In other words, if the carriers were traveling north we were on the southern rim of the circle. The other ships were supposed to stay clear of us if we didn't keep formation very well. Ordinarily we always kept formation at night by radar and you saw whether you were out of formation and getting out of position. We had no radar and on a dark night, with no moon, we could see nothing. I didn't like it and I kept slowing up and getting far behind and most of our communications, I seem to recall, were arguments with the Task Group Commander. I signalled, "I want to stay behind." He replied, "No, you've got to stay up because of danger of submarine attack." I got to the point almost where I thought I would rather have been sunk by a submarine than to have the uncertainty of a collision with others of our own forces at night. Not only did we have radio silence - you're not supposed to talk - you send blinker messages in the daytime - so our messages had to be restricted to flashing light and semaphore in the daytime with only emergency signalling at night. Staying up all night and worrying about how you were doing became a big strain for all the deck watch. It seems silly in retrospect - I guess I shouldn't have worried about it, but I did.

We were also isolated in effect, in many ways, from the news. We only had a few radios that could copy on the broadcast, Morse code, and there were no news broadcasts by voice. So we knew little about what was happening about the invasion of the Philippines - whether good or bad.

Anyway it was a long voyage back to the Surigao Strait and out into the Pacific again. Near Leyte we anchored for a day or so and then joined another carrier that had been damaged considerably in the Lingayen landings. The two of us went back to San Francisco for repairs at reduced speed because the other ship had hull damage. In San Francisco I was detached from the MANILA BAY.

Miss Kitchen: You spoke of it being a long trip. Do you remember how long?

Admiral Lee: From Lingayen Gulf down through the straits it was about three days, and then about twenty days across the Pacific. But once we were out to sea we weren't in any difficulty.

Miss Kitchen: I'm sure everyone was completely exhausted.

Admiral Lee: No. If the ship isn't operating planes there are many people who have little to do in the way of passing ammunition, moving planes and gear around, fixing up this and that, fueling the planes. They don't get tired; mostly they get bored. The engineering people and the deck watch standers work as usual. I got a lot of reading and writing done.

You asked if I could see the faces of the pilots that were attacking and the answer is no. But the pilot of the plane that went into our hangar deck and exploded was blown out of his seat and back up through the hole in the flight deck he had created by his crash. He landed some distance away on the flight deck, virtually intact, but pretty badly banged up.

Miss Kitchen: Alive?

Admiral Lee: No, very dead, but he wasn't terribly mutilated. We inspected him. It was quite interesting because he wore the ceremonial trappings that the kamikaze pilots used. He had a Japanese flag wrapped around his waist with some inscriptions on it saying in effect, "This life was given for the fatherland," and in very high sounding terms apparently. He had a scarf tied around his head which had a lot of good luck inscriptions and parting good wishes from friends such as, "You're going off to die, fella, good luck," that type of thing. He had a small Japanese military sword tied around his waist which was purely ceremonial because there was certainly not much occasion for his having to use it. The military sword of the Japanese naval officer is only about eighteen inches long - it's sort of like a long dagger. It's a badge of authority, not a weapon, just as we use our swords in the U. S. Navy.

Miss Kitchen: This was in addition to a regular uniform?

Admiral Lee: Yes. He had no uniform, just a flight suit. He was a young boy. I shipped the flag back to the Naval Academy Museum. I think it was displayed there for awhile, but they have many of those.

I also sent back the national ensign, the battle flag of the MANILA BAY, which was flying from our bridge properly when all this started. I thought it was quite unusual as a national ensign because all that was left of it was the little canvas strip that binds the pole side of the flag with the brass grommets in it. That was all that was left. All the rest of it had been burned off by the hot flame of the explosion, so the flag itself had disappeared - little bits of carbony strings coming out of this canvas binding was all that was left. I sent that back as the battle flag of MANILA BAY. I don't think they displayed that either.

Miss Kitchen: It was really, in spite of the loss of life, almost a miraculous situation.

Admiral Lee: It was good luck in lots of ways.

Miss Kitchen: It was good planning on your part. It was intelligent use of the facilities you had, talking to the men from the other ship and taking advantage of what they had to say.

Admiral Lee: I think any other person of my background and training would have done about the same thing. It's a matter of chance. Sometimes you get credit for being at a certain place at a certain time more than doing what you did at the time.

Miss Kitchen: Were there any sound effects during the time of this kamikaze attack?

Admiral Lee: Yes. When the Jap planes went into their final dives and were heading right at you, you could see the machine gun flames coming out of their machine guns and knew they were shooting at you though you couldn't hear them. Then there was a slight lapse of time and you heard an awful racket around the bridge. These were the machine gun bullets hitting the steel of the ship and it made an awful clatter before you realized whether or not you were hit. But that was just a matter of a split second or two. Then there was an awful loud bang when the bombs and the gasoline in the airplane all exploded, and that was deafening. In fact it did deafen several people who suffered ruptured ear drums. Of course other ships around us were firing their guns, too.

Miss Kitchen: So you were happy to get back to San Francisco for more reasons than one?

Admiral Lee: Yes. I was able to communicate with my wife-to-be in New York, and she was able to come out to San Francisco. The day we arrived we were married, which had an unusual circumstance attending it in a way. Her father was a judge on the Supreme Court of the state of New York, and if it hadn't been for his judicial assistance we would have had to comply with the California state laws which required a four days wait between the application for the marriage license and the marriage. He asked a judge of the Supreme Court of California to waive this provision as a matter of judicial courtesy, and he did. After he did that I said, "Can you tell us the name of a good preacher, close?" He said, "Well, no, I don't think I can, but as a judge I am qualified to perform a marriage." So he did that too right there in his chambers. It was in the Federal Court House in San Francisco, very legal.

We hired a car but we had forgotten about getting enough gas coupons, ration coupons, so we ran out of gasoline and had a terrible time getting to where we had hoped to go in Santa Barbara, otherwise no problems.

Miss Kitchen: How long were you on leave?

Admiral Lee: We had about a seven day honeymoon, but the ship was going in for major repairs and shortly thereafter, I was detached and ordered to be the Chief of Public Information for Admiral Nimitz, the Commander-in-Chief of the Pacific Ocean Area.

This happened, I suppose as many little things happen in life, because at the Naval Academy I had been interested in writing and drawing. One of my pals in working on the Lucky Bay and the Log with me was named H. B. (Min) Miller and he was the Chief of Information to Nimitz. The Secretary of the Navy wanted him to come back and be the Chief of

Information of the Navy. Nimitz told Miller, "You can go, but first you'll have to get me another man in a hurry." "Min" remembered me from our midshipmen days, we'd seen very little of each other in the interim, and gave Nimitz my name. Nimitz accepted it and before I knew it I had orders to that job, without being consulted. I felt very unqualified for it and probably was, but I went.

After my pleasant interlude in California, I flew to Guam to join Admiral Nimitz's staff. I found that I was the Mother Superior to about two hundred odd members of the American and foreign press who were accredited to Nimitz in the Pacific Ocean Area, and that this aspect of my job would occupy a large part of my time thenceforward in meeting the requirements of the press both legitimate and illigimate; personal and official, reasonable and unreasonable, worthwhile and not worthwhile at all.

The Guam headquarters was built on the top of a large hill and consisted of a large number of jumbo quonset huts for the most part. The quarters of the very senior officers were a few bungalow type buildings on the rim of this hilltop overlooking the sea and a magnificent view. The one occupied by Nimitz and Admiral Sherman, who was then his operations chief, was the center of the higher eschelon social life, including the visiting big-wigs who came to Nimitz' headquarters in the progress of the war.

I had one room in a nearby jumbo BOQ with other officers on the staff. I had charge also of what amounted to another jumbo BOQ which served as a hotel for the correspondents that were in Guam at the time. This was not a very large one, but rarely more than a hundred of the two hundred and forty or so correspondents accredited to Nimitz were in Guam at one time. The others were out on assignments to other places. They would make Guam their headquarters, and they would go and visit other units frequently. It was a very itinerant group.

We had a number of female correspondents who lived in the nurses' quarters, and they were something of a problem. There weren't many of them, six or eight, and they changed quite frequently, but they had peculiar angles that they wanted to cover from the woman's point of view of the war. They always had wiley ways of accomplishing their aims. We only had one way of discipling the correspondents out there, and that was to revoke their license to be there and send them home. We were loath to do this, of course, and in my tour of duty, although it had been done several times before I arrived, only one person's license was revoked and that was one of the women correspondents. She subsequently became very well known as a prominent writer. She was a very aggresive correspondent in the Pacific. The reason we sent her back was that during the invasion of Okinawa she went ashore with a special permit which said she had to be back on the hospital ship on which she was quartered at a certain time. Instead of that she spent four days and nights going from foxhole to foxhole getting first line experiences and with a phony pass that she had made up which let the people that she was visiting think that it was all legitimate and authorized by me.

Miss Kitchen: What was she representing?

Admiral Lee: She was a newspaper girl.

The usual routine for accommodating the press on big operations was to announce it in advance and then provide billets for the correspondents to go with various units that were going to take part in that operation. They usually volunteered and made some of the arrangements themselves, but this always became a thorny problem because some billets were considered to be superior press-wise, some were very inferior. All the correspondents considered themselves worthy of having the superior billets. They refused to divide the available billets up among themselves because seemingly the man with the poor billet would be charged by his boss at home with not being sufficiently agressive in the in-fighting for a goodie. So it usually fell to me to assign them and then to listen to the complaints from the correspondents and frequently from their bosses, and do the best we could about them.

We had quite a number of very fine newspaper men and radio people in the staff of Admiral Nimitz' Public Information section. Barry Bingham was one of them. He was our officer in charge of magazine matters. He was the editor and publisher of the Louisville Courier Journal. We had several top publishers, executives of big press chains, editors, and so forth, who were coming through as visitors, but a number of prominent press people were in uniform and working as PIOs, so this made it much better than it would have been otherwise. They were the ones that recommended the assignments and then I was able to say, "Well, this was done by a man who's wearing a uniform but he's just a member of the press like you, and he's a much better judge of where they should be than I would be, so I don't see why I should change his recommendation to me." Be that as it may, it was a continuing problem and pressures were often exerted from the publisher at home. They would complain to the Secretary of the Navy and the White House and whatnot, that their people were not given the proper facilities to cover the matter in the manner in which they thought they should be treated.

Miss Kitchen: How did you handle that type of thing?

Admiral Lee: We just said we'd do the best we can with what we had and that's all there was to it. We never had any problems really from it, but it was just one of the irritations of life that was continually with us.

The only operations that were to take place after my arrival of any significance were the invasions of Iwo Jima and Okinawa, and of course the preparations for Operation Coronet, which was the planned invasion of the Islands of Japan.

In addition to the regular press we had a large group of visitors who came through as guests of this or that - SecNav guests that were usually publisher types or people of prominence. It was one of my tasks to send them on trips and show them around and see that they were escorted. They were usually men of substance and we liked to have them. The American people got a much better impression of what was really going on when the boss publisher had had a chance to look at it and was able to censor some of his own people's writings. Henry Luce was out there, and I showed him around on Okinawa during the fighting there. Many editors of papers came on trips like that. I took them through Okinawa and visited Iwo Jima and around the installations in Guam, which were numerous and extensive. They all seemed to appreciate it. People of that caliber were usually quartered in Admiral Nimitz' guest house, which was the next cottage to his. I was usually invited along as the PIO to whatever entertainment or social get togethers they had.

We had representatives of almost every angle of the press and radio. There were some people for instance that were only interested in such things as, "How is the food service going on? I represent the Food Services Management Magazine." All they wanted to do was inspect messes and get news stories out of messes - how the frozen food was doing.

One of the most lovely people in Guam was the representative of Vogue Magazine, who wanted the woman's angle on everything. Carl Mydans, a photographer of Life Magazine and his wife, Sheffey Mydans were both there as accredited correspondents. They were both unusually fine people - intelligent, interesting, capable, highly talented, and thoroughly gentlemanly in everything they did. There were others who didn't match up to those standards. They all wanted personal stories with the top people. Everybody wanted to interview Nimitz or one of the other top people, or something of that sort, for two hours exclusive with nobody else present. This was always hard to handle.

Admiral Nimitz' personal habit was to get up about six o'clock in the morning and take a hike for exercise up in the hills in back of our camp. He was a rugged athlete himself and he would walk a fast pace and the trails were very rough. He would often ask a staff officer to go along just to talk to him while he was walking. I had to go on several such walks and they sure pooped me out. However, I proposed to Admiral Nimitz, in response to suggestions from the press, that he might take a correspondent with him occasionally, and he said he wouldn't mind. So I got a list of correspondents to make these early morning walks. Before long I found myself saying, "I have no correspondent to go with you this morning, Admiral, because those that went yesterday had such blistered feet and were so exhausted that they said to their friends, "you'll never make it."

Incidentally, Sheffey Mydans went on such a walk with him and she claims he walked at just the same pace, and she said she had no trouble keeping up with him and she'd like to go again.

While I was in Guam, working for Nimitz, the atom bombs were dropped on Nagasaki and Hiroshima. Manhattan Project, which developed the bomb, as everybody knows now, was highly secret, although a stupendous undertaking. I, as the Public Information Officer of Nimitz, under whose aegis this bombing was to be conducted, knew absolutely nothing about it up to the time it was dropped. Neither did anybody else on the staff on Guam know, with the exception of three officers. One of them was Admiral Sherman, his Operations Officer, one was Admiral McMorris, his Chief of Staff, and one of them was a captain, the officer in charge of the ordnance section of the staff who had to make some of the technical arrangements. Nimitz and those three were the only people that knew in advance that there was a bomb and we were going to use it.

I awoke one morning, turned on my little bedside radio for the armed forces radio news, and started shaving, and all of a sudden I was lathered, literally and figuratively, because a newscaster was stating as a fact that a hugh bomb of unheard proportions had just been dropped on Nagasaki, that it was the most terrific thing that was ever done. Truman's voice came on the air to explain why he had authorized it. After listening a few mintes, I rushed into my clothes thiking that all

Guam and all of the Pacific Fleet was going to be listening to this story. I was convinced that it was another one of these invasions from Mars that had paralyzed New Jersey about three years beforehand. I was sure it wasn't true, and that I had better get to Nimitz and get him to a microphone right away and say, "Settle down boys, this is all a news event." So I double timed the one hundred and fifty yards to Admiral Nimitz' house all up-hill and found him shaving. I told him while gasping for breath that he should do this. He said, "Settle down, Fitz, no problem. It's all true." Then he told me that up to this moment he had not been able to tell anybody and nobody else knew about it, but it was true and we had done this, and that we were going to do another one too.

Miss Kitchen: Did he give you an reaction?

Admiral Lee: No. It seems to me that his principal aim seemed to be to calm me down. I was very excited about the thing. I didn't believe it until he said it was true. Anyway it did cause a good deal of consternation.

Earlier I had met Admiral Parsons (he was on the AUGUSTA in China with me and we used to play tennis together). He was the chief ordinance expert who had actually developed the atomi bomb as a weapon, and he was assigned as the bomb commander of the ENOLA GAY, the plane that dropped the bomb. He had come early to Guam as part of the party that made the arrangements at the airfield on nearby Tinian. I knew he was in Guam, and I saw him at Tinian, but I didn't know why he was there, and it never occurred to me to ask him. There were all kinds of visiting officers coming through. I knew he was there on ordnance matters because he was a top ordnance scientist.

The press, of course were at a high pitch - frenzy is perhaps the better word. They wanted to examine everything and interview everybody connected with the project, and that was not being permitted. This was one of those crunches we experienced from time to time - to tell the press that they couldn't know any more than we told them at the moment and that was it, period. They'd say, "We'll have your scalp for this all right." We'd say, "Yes, our scalps grow back quite quickly. It's all right with us."

Miss Kitchen: Did you have daily press conferences, daily briefings?

Admiral Lee: Yes. We had a daily briefing in which I participated. Admiral Nimitz had a staff conference every morning at eight-thirty at his desk. He had a very large office. I would say it measured about forty by fifty feet. Half of one side was taken up by a sort of a grandstand with about four or five tiers of seats, a little amphitheater type of thing. Admiral Nimitz' desk occupied one quarter of the other half, and the other quarter was a presentation theater for anybody using props and things like that to explain any particular thing under discussion - maps, charts, and so on. Admiral Nimitz had a list of people who were authorized to come automatically to his staff conference in the morning. This meant that you could come and were expected to come, but it also was his policy that anybody who wanted to bring another staff officer for any reason could do so by checking in with the flag lieutenant beforehand and making sure that this was all right with the intelligence people. This permitted me often to bring visitors and press men and regular correspondents into Nimitz' staff meetings when the agenda did not include anything of any particular security angles. These weren't frequent occurrences, but whenever we got one like this I usually tried to have some members of the press go along with me to the press conference, and this was useful. Right after Nimitz's conference the same intelligence briefers that gave the staff their morning intelligence briefing - all about everything that had happened in the last twenty-four hours, where all the forces were and what they were doing - this same staff and I conducted a press briefing for the press, describing all the operations of the past twenty-four hours.

I might explain a little bit of the background of the upper echelons of the warriors fighting in the Pacific. CINCPOA, Commander in Chief, Pacific Ocean Areas, was Admiral Nimitz, whose headquarters were in Guam. CINCSOWESPAC was General MacArthur, whose headquarters were in various places as he marched northward toward the islands of Japan. In the latter stages of the war, after the termination of the war in Europe, the Twentieth Air Force, the Strategic Air Command under the command of General LeMay came to Guam. His headquarters were on Guam Island and his principal forces were based on Saipan and Tinian, neighboring islands, and on Iwo Jima after that was captured. These three people were each independently responsible to the Joint Chiefs of Staff for the conduct of the war. Admiral Nimitz had two hundred or more press correspondents accredited to his area and was their boss while they were there. General MacArthur had a corresponding number which were with his headquarters, sometimes more, sometimes less - not a constant population, some coming, some going all the time. When General LeMay came to Guam he apparently wanted at first to bring a third group of correspondents accredited only to him. Since the Navy, under Nimitz, had already established very large press and radio facilities there and it was a going organization, it was decided that the Navy would continue to run all of the CINCPOA correspondents, and that those who wanted to could have a double accreditation to General LeMay. General LeMay ran his separate operations briefings at his headquarters which were about a twenty or thirty minutes drive from the CINCPOA headquarters.

Inevitably in the eyes of the public and the armchair strategists, as well as in the Joint Chiefs of Staff, the operations of these three commanders were destined, as we approached Japan, to be merged into one commander. This didn't quite suit the Strategic Air Command, who felt that they should be separate in any event, but it was certainly a feeling between Nimitz and MacArthur they would finally combine forces under one commander. This was expected right along by both of them and the determination of who it would be was never formally announced to the best of my recollection before the end of the war. There was some doubt as to how it was to be handled in those last months before the end of the war. The consenus in the staff was that it would be MacArthur with Nimitz in support, and that MacArthur would be the supreme commander going ashore in Japan and would also become SCAP, Supreme Commander Allied Powers in Japan, after the war, which he did. Of course, we never did actually invade Japan.

The press corps of MacArthur's forces and the press corps of Nimitz' forces and those who were also working mostly with LeMay seemed to be obsessed with trying to bring up arguments between these three commanders as something that was newsworthy and a basis for a good news story. They would try always to ask questions, take actions, write stories, which exacerbated the relationships between the three leaders, although they would be the last to admit that they did.

As the Public Information Officer, I was also the chief censor of the Pacific Ocean Areas, and General Mac Arthur's Public Information Officer was the chief censor for his forces. This sytem was criticized by the press - that we were at the same time the Public Information Officer trying to pump it out, and also the Security Officer (censor) saying what you couldn't pump out. But it worked in both areas, and I'm sure in retrospect that it was sound. We had to censor many remarks, inferences, things out of dispatches that were filed for transmission back to the United States. We got into the sticky business of freedom of the press - what they could say and what they couldn't say. The Press would say, "Isn't it true? It doesn't effect our security. It isn't a question of national security." They were often right, but their stories were damaging to the morale of the troops and were against the policies of the actual commanders, and so it was our job to try and keep these things toned down. This often became a problem. It's easier to deal with it in war than it is in peace.

Additionally, each of the PIO staffs of these three commanders - the public information officers, in uniform, - consciously or unconsciously, were anxious to show the best aspects of the operations conducted by their particular commander. This was all tangled up with Air Force, Army and Navy and arguments and relationships about roles and missions in national security. It made for an interesting situation in which the PIOs had a hard time trying to prevent things from being made worse by reporters who wanted to elaborate and speculate and exacerbate about things in ways which were just grossly untrue sometimes, although hard to prove to be untrue, and which often had a relationship to the roles and missions issue.

Miss Kitchen: Would they try to create sometimes?

Admiral Lee: Some of them. They would write something which they knew would create a problem and then fight for their right to say it. If I may so, at this moment in 1970, it is incredible to me that we went through most of the Korean War as successfully as we did without a formal censorship and that we've gone through all of the Vietnamese War with what practically amounts to no censorship at all. It is my personal feeling, based on my experiences in Korea and in the Pacific in World War II, that our problems in Vietnam have been magnified, increased in intensity in many many areas by the fact that no censorship exists and the press are free to report anything that they want to and to seek out and record, and report anything they want to in Vietnam. In so doing, they do not, because of their own instincts and upbringing, bring about an objective picture of the whole. It's I think, a tragedy that this is allowed to go on, but it is going on and it has many defenders and now that we've once done it this way I suppose we'll never be able to fight any war in the future without having it again. I regret that this is the case. It does not reflect the true picture of the war to the citizens of our country.

Be that as it may, we had some problems along those lines. General Diller was the Public Information Officer for General MacArthur; his intelligence officer was General Willoughby who exerted a considerable influence in the public information field in General MacArthur's staff. I'm not positive right now, but I believe Diller was under Willoughby in the staff wiring diagram of General MacArthur's headquarters. General Diller and I had no problems. Basically General MacArthur and Nimitz had no policy problems along these lines. I can speak for Admiral Nimitz in saying that he went out of his way all of the time to say to the members of the press that he had no problems with General MacArthur, and these people that wanted to make him appear to have them were not doing their nation a good service.

I can remember one thing which I will paraphrase for you. Once a reporter wrote something nasty as being Nimitz' view of something that MacArthur was doing (which we had censored). Admiral Nimitz called him and me in and said, "If you print one word of anything like that, now or ever, I will personally see that you are emasculated, and you will never set foot in this ocean area again." He didn't use exactly those words — his were unprintable — but that's what he said.

Miss Kitchen: Was he more direct than that?

Admiral Lee: Yes, he was more direct than that - more lyric, more graphic. And he said the same things in much nicer ways to many people when they would make efforts along this line. The same thing is true of his relationships with General LeMay. I cannot speak for General LeMay and General MacArthur so much, although I attended a great many of General LeMay's press conferences. I frequently was there and was expected to be there much of the time. His PIO officer, General August Kissner, and I always were on the best of terms also. I happened to know him from a long friendship starting in China.

Other problems arose between the members of the press accredited to General LeMay and those accredited to Admiral Nimitz. The Navy was known as the silent service and we always kept all our ship operations very quiet. We would do everything to prevent the location of a ship or its future destination or anything like that from becoming known. So when a bunch of ships did something, we would never say who was there and what they did until it was all over and they were back in some other place. This delayed the press release date sometimes by weeks or at least many, many days. Most of the operations ashore were an entirely different category. The minute it happened, the MacArthur headquarters, or when our forces were ashore, we in the Pacific Ocean Area were able to put it out right away and the press had something fresh in the way of news.

The correspondents for General LeMay were very aggressive in being able to report things as they happened. And the correspondents who were principally reporting mostly on naval news were always complaining about the differences in handling these problems. The press releases for the bombing raid on Japan from the Twentieth Air Forces were all written out in advance, giving all the names, the number of planes, the route they would take, what the mission was, photographs of the city which was to be hit, all were written out just as if it had already happened. A complete package was prepared for the correspondents with blank spaces in a few places. When they got the radio signal from the pilot of the lead plane "bombs away," the blanks were filled in, the time and a comment on the weather or something of that sort, and off it went in the AP wires and was in the headlines all over America within a couple of hours. A corresponding naval engagement would be in within a couple of hours plus two weeks. The correspondents used to say to Nimitz and me, "You've got to do something. This is terrible. What they are doing isn't quite right." The correspondents who were working with General LeMay said, "This is just fine.. There's nothing dishonest and nothing wrong."

Miss Kitchen: It became a major problem between Admiral Nimitz and General LeMay?

Admiral Lee: No, not between those two because the system was established and approved by the Air Force as a whole from the Air Force headquarters in Washington. Although I suggested that he might, Nimitz never made any complaints about it or anything of that sort, and General LeMay never made any particular defense of it as far as I know.

The press correspondents of the Navy and many officers in the Navy felt that the methods used by the Twentieth Air Force in reporting the bombing raids on Japan were, to say the least, misleading. When a raid was planned the background data on the targets and their significance would be given to the press on a hold-for-release basis. A little later a press release would be made describing the raid in some detail even before it was flown. There would be blanks in it to be filled in. The correspondents could and often did write their stories in advance from these releases and sometimes they were pre-transmitted to the home offices on a hold-for-release basis.

If the raid was successful the photographs were released as soon as printed, together with a short follow-up release on assessed damage. If the bombs missed a mile or the wrong target was hit, nothing further was said. The result was a continuing flow of banner headlines, front page stories in the newspapers back home. Nothing like this could be done -- whether or not it was proper - in reporting the normal land and sea operations. So a misleading impression was created in the public mind about the role and effectiveness of strategic bombing. This irked many people and was a problem for me in handling complaints of people who were mad about it, including people in uniform. I was mad too, still am to a degree.

Miss Kitchen: Do you think this was the beginning of the publicity that the Air Force has always been so strong for?

Admiral Lee: I don't think it was the beginning by a long shot, but I think it was one phase of it. They were dedicated and sincere in their feelings that an awful lot of lives were being wasted unnecessarily by ground troops and naval forces in the war, and that the war would be won more quickly and much better by putting more resources into strategic air power. For most of their careers most Strategic Air Command officers had been trying to prove and advance the validity of this theory, not only to America as a whole, not only to the Army and Navy, but also to a large part of the Air Force who weren't in Strategic Command and weren't in control of the Air Force either. SAC was in control.

Miss Kitchen: Did Admiral Nimitz meet with the correspondents often?

Admiral Lee: Oh yes. He would hold occasional conferences. He would come to their morning briefings sometimes when I would ask him to, and other leading officers of the staff would be there lots of times. Admiral Sherman was there almost all the time. He was a very articulate man, had a very fine command of English, was a very good man to have from a press point of view. He was frank and had a nice personality. Admiral McMorris was a fine naval officer too, but had less ability to project his qualities to the press in a charismatic way. He was a capable man, but not one who could run for president on the basis of his T.V. appearances, if they'd had T.V. in his time, which they didn't. Admiral Sherman was a very effective man in that field.

The invasion of Iwo was well handled in the press. It was all very carefully worked out beforehand. The press section alone of the operation order for one of these major invasions was a volume about an inch and a half thick which had to be argued out and worked out in great detail. Of course many people will say too much detail, but as each operation went along you found things that went wrong which could have been very bad, and so you made an effort to do something in the next one to prevent its recurrence. This resulted obviously and rightly in too much paper work, but it had its merits too, and probably if we had it all to do over again based on the same amount of information accreting as you went along, you'd do it the same way all over again — I don't know.

Miss Kitchen: Did you have to write that?

Admiral Lee: It was my responsibility that it was written. A lot of people wrote it. I wrote some of it and I signed it.

I have the greatest admiraltion for a great many people in the press corps in the field. I became firm friends with many of them, have known them through the years, still know them and have enjoyed the privilege. The great majority are extremely fine and capable people. There's always a lunatic fringe at the bottom of every organization and even with war time restrictions on accreditations you get some press wierdies to deal with. They can be troublesome while waving the freedom of the press banner at full strength all the time and using the implied threat of "I'll damage you by what I can write unless you let me write what I want in this case." It was a factor.

Miss Kitchen: Were you ever threatened?

Admiral Lee: Well yes, not in person. I was aware many times of people saying, "Unless you give us what we want in this particular situation right now, you certainly aren't going to expect to get a sympathetic story from us in the future," things of that sort. Of course you never acceded to that and you never really suffered much from it, but you did suffer in sometimes having some of the more reasonable press on the side of their less reasonable confreres. They did this, seemingly, from the point of view that it's a press issue and we in the press must all work for these things which in a censored war are sometimes antithetical, the aims of the press and the military are working in opposition to some degree. Basically not, but there's what you might call an adversary situation.

I became a PIO later in Washington, and I can give you a prime example of that at it worst. Each time Mr. Truman flew to his summer White House at the Naval Station in Key West, Florida, a separate plane went down carrying the press who would stay with him while he was there. I, as a PIO in the Navy Department, was made aware that it was the Navy's turn to take the press down, and that the Air Force and the Army had taken people down beforehand, and that they gave the press much better treatment, and unless I did something about improving the Navy treatment we would hear about it. Well, it all boiled down to what they wanted was three or four times the amount of liquor which the Navy, as host, had provided for their health and comfort while down there in Key West. If we met their demands it would all come out of our own pockets in the PIO outfit, even though the screws were screwed on awful tight, and they didn't get what they asked for. This is an extreme case, but this was the White House correspondents, right at the top, and they were men who should have known better. It wasn't done in the name of all of them; it was done in the name of the screwball fringe at the bottom that you have to suffer with.

The invasion of Okinawa was long drawn out. Our troops landed on the western shores of the northern part of the island of Okinawa and, unknown to us, the Japanese knowing we were coming had withdrawn completely into the southern part of the island to make their stand down there. This they did, a very long and bloody stand. We went ashore unopposed, to our astonishment, and for the first three days ashore, almost, we were probing, probing, probing, and there was practically no battle action. As PIO I had the problem of knowing that there was going to be an awful lot of fighting of the worst sort and we didn't want too many of the press ashore until we had more information, so we got into a lot of hassles about how many of the press would be allowed ashore each day to visit the front line trying to hunt news in the probing process. We always let a selected few people go in early, mostly those in the wire services, so that if something significant happened it would be reported back and everybody would get it. But they didn't want that — they all demanded to get ashore at once and to stay there. This was quite an issue, but fortunately from the point of view of the PIO, at least, at one stage of the fighting we held the top of a hilly area and a lot of tough fighting was going on in the plain down below. By standing on top of the hill in our own territory you could get a panoramic view of people battling. You might get only a tiny glimpse of a man running every once in a while, but you'd see an awful lot of smoke and heard the guns being fired, and bombs being dropped from airplanes, so it was quite a grandstand show, nice to write about. The minute we got to that situation everybody was happy. They could go up and write reams about what they saw. "I was there at the firing line," and that kind of thing in the lead. I don't want to appear too critical of the press, but the PIO does see it from a different angle from the ordinary newspaper reader sees it sometimes. I come back always to the fact that there were so many wonderful people among them.

I can remember I took three newspaper publishers – one of them was the publisher of the Brooklyn Daily Eagle, one was of the Arizona Star, and another big publisher – to that hilltop in Okinawa. These were ex-reporters who had become tops in their fields. You should have seen the dispatches they immediately let go – "On the firing line in Okinawa. Your publisher was there and says ..." It's in the blood and it's good. It's part of the game.

We had all the press annexes made for the invasion of Japan and we knew where the correspondents were going to go. We were ready to detail them by name to ships and so forth, and go through the same old battles of trying to get them acceptably assigned. The atomic bomb accelerated everything, and things rapidly deteriorated and the peace came about. So we were spared the problem.

Then it became known that the surrender would take place in Tokyo Harbor, that it would be on the battleship MISSOURI, which was Halsey's flag ship at the time, and would become

Nimitz' flag ship for the occasion, MacArthur would receive the surrender with Nimitz, there would be representatives of all the Allied Nations who had participated in the war in the Pacific, and it would take place on such and such a day.

When all that became known everybody within two thousand miles in the press wanted to be there, and since Nimitz was the host and I was his PIO I had the problem of deciding who could go and where they would sit when they were there. It wasn't a happy prospect. We got a press committee together. Then, with their help, figured out how many people could sit anywhere or hang by their toenails or eyelashes anywhere on the rigging of the MISSOURI, and see the surrender deck. Then we had to categorize them, which was a common practice. You gave top precedence to the three wire services and to the three principal radio networks. Then came people from the top big dailies - New York Times, Washington Post, London Times, papers like that - based partly on the size of the circulations. But there were hundreds more who wanted to be there than we had space for. We finally had an agreement whereby we allocated so many seats to MacArthur, and so many to Nimitz, based on the average number of accredited press correspondents each had had in recent months. Then we agreed on the priority for the wire services and the big papers. If MacArthur had a top New York Times man and Nimitz had a New York Times man that didn't mean both of them could sit in the front row on top of the turret looking right down on the ceremony — one of them would have to take a back seat somewhere. We allocated all the top priority seats and added several other categories, and then put them all in a draft lottery bowl and took out by the category the numbers, and that became the final seating plan.

Miss Kitchen: Do you remember how many seats you had to allocate?

Admiral Lee: No, but it was over three hundred. Some of them were very unsatisfactory seats, admittedly, from the start, but that's what we did anyway, hoping it would work out. We also knew that a Russian delegation would be there, but were not told whether they had any newspaper correspondents with them. We allocated four seats, just in case, and, by happenstance, they brought four people. They represented Pravda, and Izvestia, and Red Flag (the Red Army newspaper), and a Russian Wire Service. We allocated these seats on the possibility that they would come, but we didn't give them any of the top priority places because we couldn't just leave any of those vacant. Our own press was against it. Anyway, we didn't and we maybe should have.

The Russians arrived late and by the time the surrender ceremony finally started we had had all the press installed for hours, hanging on by their eyebrows in uncomfortable places

The Russian delegation, headed by Lieutenant General Kuzma Derevyanko, included four Russian press correspondents. The visiting dignitaries from the nine nations that participated all had a team of top generals and officials. The press from these nations were all in their places. When the four press correspondents from Russia showed up, I was helping to greet the Russian contingent. They had arrived with General Willoughby, who spoke Russian. I said, "We have four seats for the press, so I'll take them." General Derevyanko said, "I will take them and they will stand here with me in the Russian delegation." I said, "No, you can't do that, sir, because we have many people who couldn't even come to this ship and would have given their eye teeth to be here. Those who are here have been sitting in the press seats for hours already. These are the press from all over the world, and to have your people favored wouldn't be fair, and it would cause all kinds of trouble." "Well, it'll be all right and I'll take care of the trouble." I said, "No, you can't do this." General Willoughby was the interpreter (remember that all this dailogue had to be translated and took a good deal longer to do than what I'm saying here) and he got impatient and said, "Let them stand down there." I said, "No, sir, this is wrong. You can't do it."

Well, looking right down on the surrender scene from the MISSOURI's turret was the front row of top drawer correspondents, and many other press on a sort of grandstand behind them. They started clapping and applauding with "Bravos" every time I said anything, because I was standing up for the American press in the face of Pravda. They were mad at General Willoughby and seemed to indicate it. Things got sticky. Time was going by. They had arrived late and we were behind schedule already, so General Willoughby said, "I order you to do this." I said, "No, sir, if you ask Admiral Nimitz to order me to do it, I will. I'll take you right now to him in his cabin in there." He said, "No, I will not do that. I want you to do this." Big applause from the press when I said no. I said, "General, if these press people of your group don't go to their seats now, I will call the Marine guard and they will be taken off the platform and either escorted to their seats or they will not be present at the ceremony." Willoughby turned purple and said, "All right." The Russian then said, "Oh that's all right, fine, take them up to their seats." So that ended that, but I had the Marines there, and the Marines showed them to their seats.

Miss Kitchen: You must have gotten a big hand from the gallery.

Admiral Lee: I did. It was written up in quite a number of the papers, represented by correspondents at the ceremony.

After the ceremony was completed and the Japanese delegates had left the ship, and almost all the rest of the senior delegates had filed into the nearby Admiral's cabin, the surrender table was left out there in the middle of the open space on deck. Nobody broke ranks to swarm around it, because they were waiting for the last delegates and senior officers to leave the area. I saw then that the four press correspondents of the Russians, who had been taken up to their seats by the Marines, had sneaked down during the course of the ceremony and were standing with General Derevyanko. He and the four press correspondents, one of whom had a camera, rushed out and turned the table around ninety degrees to get a better angle. Then the whole Russian delegation and their press correspondents sat on the surrender table with their arms akimbo - the victorious, "we just won the war" picture. They had their pictures taken laughing and joking, and then the Russians left, and I never knew what happened to the correspondents.

Mind you, the Russians had entered the war just six days before this, and their adamant and brazen insistence that things be done just the way they wanted to do it was a real eye-opener with portents for Russia's future conduct, of just how they were going to act in the future, and it is just about what they have been doing ever since. Those who saw this act on the deck of the MISSOURI would never have dreamed that it would be their national policy from then on, but so it has been.

Miss Kitchen: Also it proved that you knew how to deal with them, and that's the way they had to be dealt with, even though they made an end run afterwards.

Admiral Lee: I hadn't thought of that angle, but I do think that if we had more often done much the same thing as I did on that occasion in subsequent affairs around the globe, we'd be a lot better off. It was an interesting interlude.

Shortly after that I had another sidelight on what makes news. All the correspondents wanted to go immediately ashore, and see how Japan looked when the shooting had stopped. We weren't quite ready to have them race in to see who could be first to see this and that. I had been ashore already and was trying to figure out arrangements, and we were in the process of setting up a press headquarters on shore at the Yokosuka Naval Station.

The ANCON, the ship that the press were berthed in was brought in to the dock and we were in business for sight-seeing. It worked out all right. Enough of them got ashore pretty soon, and there were no difficulties that I remember particularly. But I was surprised that top priority seemed to be the race to be the first to interview Tokyo Rose. I went up in the first press party that went into Tokyo to help some of them find Tokyo Rose. We went to the big press building which the press knew about from previous years in Tokyo, much like our press headquarters in Washington. We went there and talked to the top people who were in the building, and pretty soon they produced Tokyo Rose, and some of them interviewed her. I wasn't present at the interview, but the one that said he got the best answers said he got them because he was able to give her six pairs of nylon stockings, which he knew she would want and which he had purchased for this purpose long beforehand in Guam.

As I mentioned earlier I knew Tokyo pretty well, having lived there a good deal, so I toured several groups of correspondents around Tokyo showing them things that I thought would be interesting for them to see, and looking at the battle damage, which was pretty awful.

I might make a side note for history here. On the occasion of one of my visits from Guam to MacArthur's headquarters in Manila I observed that the devastation from the American bombing attacks on Manila was pretty grim. A great many buildings were knocked down and rubble was all over the place. This was considerably after - several months after - the bombing had occurred, but the Filipinos were still standing around in long lines with their arms outstretched asking for doles and handouts - food and what have you. Not one rock had been put back on top of another. There had been little or no attempt to clean up the mess so far as I could see. They didn't seem to be doing anything useful.

Well, we drove up through Yokohama and on to Tokyo through one of the big areas that had been practically wiped out flat by the fire bomb and other bomb raids, but the street cars were running; all the rubble was piled up in neat little walls. Along the sidewalks they piled up rocks into bins which served as little gardens about three feet across and about six feet long. Vegtables were planted in them. The streets were clean, and the places where the people were living were hovels in the sense that they were made of paste board and straw matting and pieces of corrugated tin, all was twisted and bent, but they were neat and clean and well swept. The place was running and nobody was asking for handouts from anybody that was visible, at least to me as a casual tourist. This difference between the Malay and the Jap made a tremendous impression on me.

Miss Kitchen: How long was this after the surrender ceremony?

Admiral Lee: Three or four days. I had seen some of it before the surrender ceremony when I was ashore, but this made an impression on a lot of people. It did on me.

The other newsworthy anecdote that I can recall was that the correspondents all wanted to go ashore with Admiral Halsey and see him ride on the Emperor's white horse. That came number two after interviewing Tokyo Rose. When Admiral Halsey first went ashore, I went with him and they had a press drawing to see what press people would come with us - there were only five or six, we didn't advertise it much. We went into the Tokyo Yokosuka Naval Station, a nice place with many stone buildings, damaged very little by the war. We wandered around and the press sent scouts out and were offering money and cigarettes to anyone who could find a white horse somewhere for Halsey to ride. Halsey had no intention of riding on a white horse. He told me beforehand, "You damned well know I'm not going to do that."

Halsey is a rather dramatic flamboyant type of person and he had never been in Japan before. He was extremely impressed by the minature size of all the western style things in the officers club of the Yokosuka Naval Station. The furniture was mostly western style furniture in many parts of it and all in a very small scale, as is almost all western furniture in Japan. I traveled a lot in Pullman cars in Japan in my earlier years and I can testify that the berths from solid head to solid foot are five feet eight and a half inches. A six footer, as I am, could never stretch out.

Pointing right and left Halsey said, "These people who gave us so much trouble; and they make a little thing like this, no better than this, only this big..." He would go around kicking the under-sized tables and arm chairs and nicknacks that were notable to him only because of their small size as compared to their counterparts in our country. This, of course, was newsworthy for the correspondents - they loved it. But his reaction was interesting. He was pretty rough speaking lots of times, used plenty of profanity. He was somewhat Patton-like in these things.

Miss Kitchen: Kind of like the conqueror?

Admiral Lee: Not in that sense. It was a sense of frustration that it was the people who couldn't build a better chair and table and desk had caused us so much trouble. He didn't see why we didn't win quicker.

In looking back over my times as PIO for Nimitz, I can remember many times when I admired his handling of difficult situations. He was a very friendly outgiving person in many ways. He always made friends among all kinds of people and they admired him. Socially he was genial, pleasant, and soft spoken, quiet and modest, but he did have forces and was very direct and outspoken when he wanted to get things done that needed to be done from among his subordinates. He was also quite profane, though I never heard him utter a profane word other than in bachelor circumstances.

In Guam as the Commander-in-Chief he lived modestly, but he did have a place that was big enough to have a dinner party for as many as twenty people and the staff to handle them. I would say that on Guam on an average of two or three times a week Nimitz had guests for dinner. I attended many of these dinners, and they were usually to honor visiting friends of some distinction. This was toward the end of the war, and Forrestal was Secretary of the Navy. He was anxious to have all kinds of prominent Americans come out and see what the Navy was doing. He thought that was part of his job to make sure that more Americans, particularly in the publishing and media world, should come see with their own eyes. So we would have mixed lots of people that came to the headquarters. As the PIO, I had the general responsibility of making sure that they were welcome and had a place to live and were well treated. Questions of protocol might often have come up as to who should sit where at the Nimitz' dining table. Did the head general of the Chinese Nationalist Forces rank ahead of the president of the First National City Bank of New York? That never was an issue after the problem arose early in the game, and somebody was miffed, and I was embarrassed, because he wasn't seated right. From that time on Nimitz would always say, "We have a precedence rule for protocol here, and we hope you will go along with it because we feel that it is an old and venerable Chinese custom and a good one. The most honorable guest is the oldest. Each of the guests will please take your seats marked for guests in the order of your age. Now who is over seventy?" He started off that way, then he would seat them all according to their age in the guest seats. It disposed of all kinds of silly litle problems.

He was a magnificent raconteur and he had an infinite variety of stories. He always had an appropriate story for any occasion. Most of them were for bachelor gatherings. I can't remember any of the stories; I'm not a good raconteur.

And he wasn't a good raconteur in the sense of mimicry of a language. He never tried to give an accent to Italian stories or Jewish stories or anything of that sort, but he had a lot of salty stories. He loved to tell them, and he would string them out pretty long, but they were always funny and a propos.

He was always gracious to everybody, and nobody ever felt on any occasion, in his home or anywhere that I've ever been, that they weren't completely welcome, and just the most important guest there. He made an effort to speak to everybody, the youngest and the most junior, and so forth. He also would, on occasion, make some observations to other officers of his staff that they weren't doing enough of that.

I made a terrible boo-boo one time. It was one of the world's worst. A press correspondent made a perfectly terrible statement in a story that got through our censorship and was printed in a Washington newspaper. He had sort of circumvented the censor in doing this, but it may even have gotten in anyway. It was just nasty and it wasn't true. I never even knew about it. Someone in Washington sent it to Nimitz and he showed it to me. He was livid about it and I said, "Well, let's write a letter to the man's publisher, the head of the paper, and tell him that it was wrong and you'd like a retraction. I will write a letter from the PIO if you want it that way," which I did. But the original story appeared in the Washington Star, and I wrote to the publisher of the Washington Post. I caught the devil for that, but I deserved it.

Miss Kitchen: Did he really chew you out, what did he say?

Admiral Lee: Yes, he chewed me out, some profanity was used.

Miss Kitchen: Did he humiliate you?

Admiral Lee: No. I think he always tried to follow the rule of not bawling anybody out in public. He bawled them out privately.

Miss Kitchen: What kind of fitness reports did he make?

Admiral Lee: You only see your own. He gave me good ones, and gave me a Legion of Merit for my service under him. I don't know whether he really thought that well of me or not. I'm sure he gave very fair fitness reports.

Miss Kitchen: Did he do a lot of writing on it? Did he do it in long hand, or were they typed?

Admiral Lee: It used to be required that you write it in your own hand writing, and in those years most everybody did.

As a matter of fact the Marine fitness reports still so require it - that is the personal evaluation paragraph at the bottom of the form.

I never saw any of the fitness reports that Nimitz wrote on anybody with the exception of my own, and I don't remember if they were handwritten.

Interview # 2

Vice Admiral Fitzhugh Lee

At his home, Coronado, California   August 9, 1970

Subject: Biography   by E. B. Kitchen

Miss Kitchen: I think the last time we stopped with your detachment from Admiral Nimitz' staff in Guam.

Admiral Lee: This marked a milestone in my career, starting into a post-war life at a time when I had become more mature and was more aware of the important things that went into the management of the Navy.

Admiral Miller had been my predecessor in CincPac as the Public Relations Officer, and he had become the Director of Public Relations in Washington. He asked that I come back and serve in the Office of Public Relations in the Navy to help him in that assignment.

The problems of the Navy in those years were manifold. I was concerned principally with only two things. One was the struggle in Washington over the reorganization of the armed forces as the result of war time experience. There was a move afoot, which had started many years beforehand, to unify the armed forces, to create a separate Air Force, co-equal with the Army and the Navy, to have a single Chief of Staff, those types of things. These posed problems for the Navy internally and in our relationships with other service with the Congress, and also with the media, who were always trying to exacerbate our difficulties it seemed to me.

My second assignment, which was of interest, was that Mr. Forrestal gave me a special mission to create an advertising campaign to insure a naval reserve of over a million men. We wanted to hold on to the great pool of educated talent that we had in the Navy through the thread of a Navy Reserve in order to compensate in some respect for the terrific decrease in our numbers of ships and men at the end of the war - our total disarmament, almost - at a time when Russia and other people weren't disarming at all. One phase of this developed into a recruiting program to get a million men to sign up in the Reserve. Mr. Forrestal authorized the appropriation of something like a hundred thousand dollar contract with the J. Walter Thompson Advertising Company for the making of films, for promotional literature, for advertising means and methods, and texts which would produce the million men.

Miss Kitchen: And was this at the time you were in the Office of Public Relations?

Admiral Lee: Yes, but it was more-or-less a side duty which occupied me for about five or six months, a lot of it in New York. The J. Walter Thompson Company said that the way to do it from their soundings on marketing, research of public opinion, and so forth was to stress joining the Navy and learning a trade. This ran counter to the feelings of many of the old officers in the Navy who said, "No, that's not what we want them to do. We want them to join the Navy and help defend our country and not put in on a personal 'what's in it for me' basis, but on the basis of patriotism." This became my principal stumbling block in trying to reconcile what J. Walter Thompson thought best and the Navy, itself, thought best, and still get the million men.

Miss Kitchen: And how did you resolve that?

Admiral Lee: We didn't resolve it but we tried to compromise it, making both sides unhappy, but we did get a million men, so I guess it worked out all right.

The greater part of my duties in public relations were not direct contacts with the media or the usual things that one conceives of as being part of public relations duties, but in handling the various problems that kept coming up on the unification issue.

At that time a book was published called, "The Case Against the Admirals." It was a scurrilous book, attacking the Navy and the Navy high command for its reluctance to engage in more amalgamation, unification, integration with the other services. I had some part in our efforts to counteract "The Case Against the Admirals." At one stage of this

2 Lee - 186

I interviewed the author, William Bradford Huie, who had been a correspondent in the Pacific command when I was working for Admiral Nimitz, and whom I knew did not have the respect of most of his contemporaries in his own profession. He told me very clearly that he didn't believe a thing that he wrote in the book, but that he was paid to write it, and that he was a professional writer and a professional writer took on any assignment he was given. I think I recall his having used the words, "It's like an artist painting a portrait." He didn't like to paint sticky post card views of Grandma, making her look younger than she was, he wanted to paint a real character portrait of her, but this didn't please the family, and the family paid the bill, and the artist painted it the way the family wanted it. This is the way he wrote books.

Miss Kitchen: Did he say who told him to write it this way, or who paid him to write it?

Admiral Lee: He would not divulge who paid him to write it, but the publishing house paid the bills. I never found out who the actual funder was. Possibly it was all paid by the publishing house or individuals in it, I don't know. It was obvious that the motivation was to undercut the Navy's case in the struggles which were going on.

Miss Kitchen: Did you ever suspect that any of the other services might have had a hand in it?

Admiral Lee: Well, I think almost everybody suspected things like that of all three services. So I can't say that I or the Navy was Simon pure in that respect, but I think we had higher standards. Feelings were running high and these things were difficult to handle. Drew Pearson was also very much against us. This stems from the fact, I believe, that when Pearson and Allen were writing the Washington Merry Go Round just before the war, they decided that each would join one of the armed services during the conflict; they would then come back to write better and bigger things after the war was over. Allen was taken by the Army and made a major immediately, and put in positions of considerable prestige and power. Mr. Pearson said that he would join the Navy and the Navy said, yes, he could come in but only as a j.g. and if he didn't like it he couldn't come in. So he didn't come in, and he continued writing but with something of a sour taste for the Navy, possibly as a result of that incident. In any event, Mr. Pearson's column was very active in the internecine warfare of the services and it wasn't on the Navy's side. Mr. Jack Anderson, who was then working for Mr. Pearson, and I had several meetings in trying to bring facts into print in Pearson's column, and I did not succeed.

Miss Kitchen: Do you have any for instances?

Admiral Lee: Well, some of them came in The Case Against The Admirals, which Pearson quoted liberally. We had told him his facts were not true and we were prepared to document the truth. They went ahead and published them just the same. This, I might say, together with my experience in dealing with several hundred war correspondents in the war, quickened me in my interest in public relations and the media and their relationship to the armed forces through the years.

I kept being impressed with the quality of the top twenty percent of the press - how wonderful they were, how eight-five or ninety percent were certainly as competent and able as in any other big organization in society, but that the bottom ten percent were a bunch of rascals that were unpoliced, one hundred percent unpoliced, by their contemporaries and professional equals, or their employers. There was no way of disciplining them when they went off on a limb and said things that were untrue. Their morals were never questioned by their own profession. This is one of the prices of Freedom of the Press.

Miss Kitchen: And when they did publish it there was no action one could take against them, as I recall, to show one side, or there's no slander or libel against a man who writes an article.

Admiral Lee: I think that's true. I can give you an example, partly hearsay, partly based on observation, going back to my war experience. I was the Flag Secretary to COMAIRPAC briefly early in the war, during the Battle of Midway. Some carriers had been sunk in the South Pacific and some of the people were being brought back into Pearl Harbor on board ships. Among them was a correspondent, I think from the Chicago Tribune, I believe his name was Stanley Johnson. He came back in a destroyer, and I think he was the only press member on board the destroyer. We had a talkative skipper on that destroyer and he divulged, in ward room conversations, that we had succeeded in breaking the Japanese codes. Mr. Johnson knew that this was highly top secret, but nevertheless thought that it was so newsworthy that he had to write it. He wrote without our knowledge and it was published in the Chicago Tribune in a brief article. It would have been a terrible disaster for us if the Japanese had latched onto the fact that we had broken their codes. However, they didn't and kept on using the codes which we could read, which was a big asset to us.

However, disciplining Mr. Johnson was a horse of another color. The Navy, who had been instrumental in breaking this code, and who was at that time the principal beneficiary (the Battle of Midway being an example) sort of felt that the man should have been punished. Steps were taken to punish Mr. Johnson for this dereliction, and possibly his publisher.

The law was very clear, it still is - it provides ten years imprisonment, or ten thousand dollars fine, or both. If convicted of treason it can be even more. The case went through a great deal of undercover investigators and, in the end, was decided by Mr. Roosevelt, the President, himself. He said in effect, "We cannot try this case because it involves the question of the freedom of the press and it also would be impossible to do it without causing many problems for us in other areas in connection with code breaking that would come out as a result of this trial because he could not be tried in secret." So Johnson went free. The press didn't condemn him. He subsequently became the editor of a Santa Barbara newspaper.

This incident made a tremendous impression on me and made me feel badly about the way things went wrong for the Navy sometimes because of this irresponsible, unpunishable ten percent of the media. I tilted with that windmill for many years, but I'm no farther ahead now than I was then because the same thing still obtains. I could cite dozens of incidences.

Mr. Forrestal, who was then the Secretary of the Navy was also very deeply involved in the unification process, which eventuated in 1947 in the creation of the National Security Act of 1947. He set up a special group called the Secretary's Policy Research Group, or words like that. It was headed by Captain Tommy Robbins, in the U. S. Navy, and it was to gather the

Navy's position together for any hearings that were to be held in connection with the creation of a new national security act and a new organization in the armed forces.

Captain Robbins and I were good friends, and I was in public information and worked with him a good deal in assembling the Navy's history of our case, and gathering together all of the lumber that the Navy Department could use in building its case. This got me very much interested in the history of unification, roles and missions of the armed forces in our own country and other countries.

While I was on this duty, Mr. John Sullivan became the Under Secretary of the Navy. A good friend of mine was his aide, and had a chance to go to sea and did. He put the bee on me and I was required to change duties. This was something entirely new to me, but it had the effect of catapulting me into the top circle of officials that had been in the military at the top, which was extremely interesting. And I was very much in the stage of Alice in Wonderland for quite a number of months, perhaps all of my tour there, when I worked for Mr. Sullivan.

During the incumbency of Mr. Sullivan the 1947 National Security Act came about, and Mr. Forrestal was made the first Secretary of Defense and Mr. Sullivan was made the first Secreatry of the Navy under the new arrangement, and I continued as his aide.

These were the years when we were going through the throes of the Congressional hearings which led to the birth pains of the National Security Act. Naturally most of the top policy decisions in the Navy were percolating through the offices close to me, and although I was not in a decision making role in any of them, I was aware of them, and I think I was helpful to the Secretary.

Mr. Symington was the Secretary of the Air Force and the principal collision areas during the hearings and in the early years of the unification act were between the Air Force and the Navy over the role of aviation.

Miss Kitchen: You were a good man to be in that position.

Admiral Lee: Well, I had more background, perhaps, than many of my contemporaries. But maybe the Navy could have had a much better man there at the time.

Miss Kitchen: Do you have any recollections of strife when Mr. Sullivan did ask your advice where you thought you were helpful?

Admiral Lee: I would say that strife was pretty much the routine as concerned getting the new organization going. There were strong differences of opinion between men who were leaders in their own fields and dedicated to their own beliefs. But it was polite strife and people tried to make things work. No one, however, wanted to be a participant in a decision which would be unfavorable to his service and destined to be precedent-setting.

Miss Kitchen: There would have been no naval aviation if the Air Force had had its way, as I recall.

Admiral Lee: This was the way the Navy cased it also. We knew we were fighting for the continuance of aviation as a part of the Navy. I think the last thirty years have probably vindicated our stand, but at the time it was often nip and tuck. Many things were done which perhaps are better left off the record. The Forrestal Diaries, edited by Walter Millis, has a great deal of material about what went on, but even though it was compiled by a journalist who wanted to tell the whole story it doesn't tell it.

Mr. Symington and Mr. Sullivan, basically, were not on good terms. At cocktail parties, receptions, and official meetings, they were the best of friends, but under the surface they were bitter enemies.. I believe that Mr. Sullivan felt that Mr. Symington resorted to means and methods that were not proper. As an example, a meeting was held in Los Angeles of the Aviation Writers Association - one of their annual conventions to which they asked prominent speakers - and Mr. Symington made an address to this group. He did not know that his talk was being recorded. It wasn't planned to be recorded, and

I am satisfied personally that what I am about to relate was true because I had to investigate it.

The speaker after Symington was to be a Navy man and the Navy wanted to record his speech, and they set up a tape recorder to record it. The fellow just turned it on when Symington started just for the sake of making sure that he was getting a clear recording and that was it. That was his original motive, but after listening a while he let it run for the whole thing. Mr. Symington did not know this.

Mr. Symington departed very considerably from the text which he had presented for his speech beforehand and which had been cleared for him to make. This fact was so reported by a number of the aviation writers present, including Mr. Hanson Baldwin, who gave considerable detail in the New York Times of the things that Mr. Symington said.

This caused quite a stir because Mr. Symington's words were patently aimed at the Navy and the Navy's position. Mr. Sullivan immediately made an issue of it and Mr. Forrestal called in Mr. Symington, who said it all a pack of lives, that it wasn't ture. Then Mr. Symington said that he did not know that his speech had been recorded. Then there was a huddle at the top and the recording was played. Mr. Symington was reprimanded, but not fired, and Mr. Sullivan's feelings were ruffled and not entirely assuaged. This man in a high office of government had lied to his boss on a matter of considerable importance at the time, in effect, got to go scot-free.

This I thought was very wrong; so did others.

Miss Kitchen: I'm sure it was known among his peers.

Admiral Lee: Very few. The damage had been done. The fact that he had lied and then been trapped in it and bawled out for lying was never known to any degree, so far as I know he was never punished for it. I never had much respect for Mr. Symington after that. Everything he said was to me rather suspect, and he has said a lot of things through the years that have been harmful in my view, which I sometimes doubted the veracity of.

I liked Mr. Sullivan and my years with him were interesting and happy. I may say that I was astounded not only by the Symington incident just mentioned, but also by many other things that went on in politics - things I had been blissfully ignorant about through all of my previous lifetime. I found that I had been using a code of morals and ethics which was considerably different than those practiced in some fields of government and politics. These are all little things which the politician feels he must do, but which the moralist would say he shouldn't do.

I gave a talk recently in San Diego to a group here. It was about a year ago when the military industrial complex was being widely vilified. I had prepared a talk which I didn't use, I just talked off the top of my head. I said that I thought that this vilification of the military industrial complex was a terrible thing for the United States, especially because it wasn't based on facts. I said I couldn't be sure of the industrial side of it, but I knew from the military side that our basic creed, which is the West Point motto of Honor, Duty, Country, was strongly ingrained in all the top military people and we policed our own organization according to it. If somebody in the military didn't follow that code he was punished. And I asked them to try to recall any high ranking military officers anywhere in the world - there may have been a rare exception or two in many thousands - who had done things wrong from a moral point of view. I said that in general, they were absolutely clean and that, "I cannot find another of the professions of our society which similarly polices itself." The lawyers don't, the doctors don't the educators don't. They will not punish the bad performers, except in the most flagrant cases. To get a lawyer disbarred from practice is practically an impossibility.

Miss Kitchen: When you were aide to Mr. Sullivan, do you recall Mr. Gross from the Pacific Light and Power Company in San Francisco calling on him and reporting some information concerning the trust territories, and Mr. Sullivan asking you to fly him to New York in Mr. Sullivan's plane? Mr. Gross said you flew over Princeton and President Truman was there. There had been a note on the bulletin board that you were not to fly over Princeton that day.

2 Lee - 197

Admiral Lee: I recall the incident of flying Mr. Gross up to New York at Mr. Forrestal's request. Mr. Forrestal was a graduate of Princeton and said something about showing Mr. Gross the countryside on the way up because he, Gross, had never left the West Coast. So I took him on the scenic tour over the beautiful Green Spring Valley region outside of Baltimore, around Wilmington where the DuPont's had built mansions and marvelous parks, circled over Princeton and the Main Line of Philadelphia, and so on. It was a beautiful summer day, and these states and the green countryside were something to view from the air, much like England. When we landed in New York, Mr. Gross got out. But I must go back to say that in the small, old plane we were in you didn't have two-way communication between pilot and passenger. It was a little open-cockpit two-seater. He was in the back seat and I could talk to him, but he couldn't talk to me, so I was describing what he was looking at. When we got to New York he said, "You know I honestly never knew that they had so much irrigated land in the East." He honestly thought that all this had been irrigated because it was all green in midsummer. I probably hadn't read the bulletin board because if I had and seen it, I think I would have obeyed it.

Miss Kitchen: Mr. Gross said you were too good an aviator not to have followed the rules but there was much excitement when you flew down over Princeton, and many helicopters flying over; then you flew down to take a better look at what was going on because President Truman was there that day.

Admiral Lee: I think Mr. Gross embroidered that a bit. I don't remember that part.

To go back to my duties with Mr. Sullivan - one of the great issues of the time was the fact that Mr. Louis Johnson, who was the new Secretary of Defense after Mr. Forrestal died, convinced Mr. Truman that he could save all kinds of money in the armed forces in the post-war years by cutting out the fat. He was rapidly cutting out not only the fat, but an awful lot of the muscle. One of the big issues came up in the building of a new aircraft carrier. Congress had approved the building of the carrier, UNITED STATES, which was called a flush deck carrier because it had no super structure. Whether or not we would build any further carriers became an issue. The monies had all been appropriated for building the UNITED STATES, but Mr. Johnson unilaterally cancelled the building of the ship. Mr. Sullivan learned about it in the newspapers.

This occurred just after I had left Mr. Sullivan's employ. As a result of that particular incident Mr. Sullivan resigned as Secretary of the Navy. Admiral Dennison was then the aide to President Truman. Admiral Dennison and I had worked closely when I was working with SecNav and he was at the White House. So we were both aware of some of the problems. Mr. Sullivan's original letter of resignation, which he sent me a copy of, was to Mr. Truman. It then developed that this was a bad thing for Mr. Sullivan to do - he was still a good and respected friend of Mr. Truman and vice versa, and they were both good Democrats.

So it was worked out that Mr. Sullivan (who had something of an Irish temper) after signing, sealing, and delivering this letter to Mr. Truman had to take it back and address it to the Secretary of Defense instead of Mr. Truman, which he did. This was another one of the twists in politics that amused me.

I traveled a lot with Mr. Sullivan all over the United States, principally to naval installations. I think I was instrumental, in a minor way, in the selection of Monterey, California for the Navy's new Postgraduate School, after the decision had been made to move it out of Annapolis. Three communities in the West Coast were vying strongly to get the school. One of them was Monterey, which was offering the grounds of the old Hotel Del Monte there; one was Seattle, Washington; and one was Los Angeles. There were two other lesser contenders. The issue got very sticky from the political angle. The Navy wanted Monterey but wasn't allowed to say so in public. I told Mr. Sullivan that I thought he ought to go out and look at these sites before he made a dicision. I thought it was ridiculous for him to make a decision of this magnitude, and for political reasons, without going out and inspecting the sites because there were bound to be a lot of repercussions.

Mr. Sullivan was an ardent golfer and when I described the golf courses at Monterey he was more inclined, I think, to go and take a look. I think if he hadn't been an ardent golfer it's just possible he wouldn't have gone. But he took along a favorite golfing pal of his and went out to the West Coast and inspected the sites. It was obvious, golf courses or no, that the Monterey site was the better site. So he came back and picked it in spite of the fact that he was a close personal friend of the Senator of the state of Washington, who was pinging on him very strongly.

Miss Kitchen: Would you go back and pick up the Operations Crossroads in 1946?

Admiral Lee: That was another collateral assignment while I was basically assigned to the Office of Public Information. The Navy decided to conduct a scientific test of the effects of atomic bombs against naval shipping. A group of old Navy war ships and some captured Japanese ships and other types of military equipment were all taken to Bikini for the sake of making accurate measurements of the damage which would be inflicted by the blast, fire, and radiation damage of an atomic blast. It became a matter of great interest to the whole nation and to the whole world. Delegations, including correspondents, were invited to witness these tests from all of the nations who participated in the Pacific war, including Russia. We ended up with a hundred and sixty-eight correspondents, representing some eleven nations, almost all of them from the United States but several from Asiatic papers and one representative from Red Star, the newspaper of the Armed Forces in Russia. I was placed in charge of the public information aspects of the test. I had to get these hundred and sixty-eight people out there and keep them happy while we were there for some six weeks in the South Pacific in a non-alcoholic non-airconditioned ship in very overcrowded conditions, and hopefully bring them all back safely without radiation damage, and with their stories well told.

The first problem was to figure out how many people could be taken and then to choose the names of those who would go. This was a major operation and we were given the Navy's amphibious command ship, APPALACHIAN, which had a considerable amount of passenger space. We concluded that about a hundred and twenty-eight was the most that could be taken. The press rose in great anger and said, "Send two ships or do better." So we kept looking at the ship again, and by devoting various spaces that properly shouldn't have been living accomodations for this purpose we ended up taking a hundred and sixty-eight. In retrospect, this was a mistake because it was too crowded, too hot, and too unbearable. I only mention this because the objectivity of the news representatives is often affected by their environment in more ways than one.

Also we undertook to send back promptly by radio a great number of words by teletype and to do it quickly. This became a major issue because you could only send on so many channels and proving additional communication channels was almost impossible. Teletype transmission over long distances from moving ships was then in the early development stage and wasn't an easy thing to do. We put a great deal of effort into it and some four hundred and fifty thousand words went out in the first twenty-four hours, of which about only five percent were garbled. The authors of the garbled stories spent the next five years complaining about this. It was unfortunate.

One correspondent whose message to the Boston Daily Globe was badly garbled took a great deal of wordage in his paper to explain what a horrible mess it had been. He said it was the negligence of the naval personnel that had brought about this disaster, which was to be expected. He said other nasty things, such as that if they had only allowed the reservists, who really won the war in spite of the old line of the Navy, to be there they would have had a perfect record and so on. I wrote a letter to the publisher of the paper giving him all the facts and figures - the staff was practically all reservists, et cetera - which were quite different from those supplied by his own man. My letter was never acknowledged and the story in the paper was never corrected. This is another of my disillusionments with the press, but these are isolated incidents and you so often have so many wonderful press people to work with that you can overlook them.

Actually, my one bit of genius, if I may say so, was hitting on the idea that I would not make all the decisions as to who got priority on the messages going out and how many "takes" could be sent. Could AP send a "take" of ten words after the first bomb drop and then UP send ten words, then the

New York Times send ten words, as one of the ways of doing it? Actually on hot stories this is what is done. I said I would not make myself the arbiter of these decisions and that the press could themselves choose a committee who would arbitrate every decision regarding the choice of priorities. They tried to get out of it, but I insisted and they finally did choose a fine committee. Several well known names were on it - Bob Considine, a long time writer for AP and the Baltimore Sunpapers, was one. The members of the committee were highly regarded members of the press and they made all the sticky decisions from that point on.

I used this technique in later years successfully, too, and always with much initial protest from the press. They don't like to make these hard decisions among themselves. They want somebody else to make it, and the freedom to complain about it.

An example of the irresponsibility of the press at the Bikini Bomb Test was one of the first headlines that went out. It was picked up world-wide, and reported that the whole test was invalidated because the bomb had gone off by mistake too far away from the planned spot and much too high. This was unfortunate because public confidence in the validity of the test was destroyed. This screaming headline appeared first in the European press and was picked up from the European press before the U. S. press got ahold of it, since part of our communications were going around the world that way. But the story was wrong. The bomb went off very close to the desired ground zero, the spot we were aiming at, and at the precise altitude and at just about the precise time, which was a tremendous technical achievement. We could have expected some minor errors, which really didn't occur. The correspondents were located on the island of Kwajalein, which was some distance from Bikini, but many of our support planes were based there. These two correspondents had been allowed to ride in an Air Force airplane, and had been able to see the blast from the air. (We had quite a number of correspondents in aircraft in the air.) When they landed at Kwajalein the correspondents said that they were filing a message right away and right there. Their story said that the bomb had been way off base and way too high. My representatives there, in charge of the press at Kwajalein said, "Don't send this. We don't know this is true." They said, "The bombardier in our airplane said it was true." My man said, "That person is in no position to know if it's true, so you shouldn't send this." But it was sensational, and they insisted. I think if I had been there I would have just simply killed it and been excoriated for doing so. But my man didn't, and they sent it. Then after it was all over and the damage was done our investigation showed that we were right; these correspondents had insisted on doing this against the advice of the military commander who said they shouldn't but by crying "freedom of the press" they had sent it. I took this case to my Press Committee and said, "What are you going to do with people who do that?" We had a second test scheduled in a few weeks. I said I thought a few people ought to be sent home, at the very least. Well, the end product was that nothing was done against those correspondents and blame was imputed by anybody in the press to members of the press for doing it.

Another interesting character there was a representative of the Red Star, the Russian paper. He was very much of a gentleman, a well educated person -- his English was quite weak, but I would say he was among the more gentlemanly of the contingent present. I had many talks with him about Russia. He was a major in the Russian Army and Red Star is the official publication of the Russian armed forces. I never did see any of his accounts of the bomb -- they all went out in Russian.

In between the first test, which was the blast in the air, and the second test, which was an under water test, we had a month to kill. I tried to get the correspondents sent home and then brought back again, but one thing led to another and it wasn't done. We took them back to Hawaii for rest and recreation, but still they were a very restive, unhappy group. I couldn't blame them in many ways. My beef was that their restiveness and unhappiness with the personal accomodations and the weather were so frequently reflected in their stories, over which we had no control.

Miss Kitchen: You might indicate why these were called Bikini tests. I don't want anyone a hundred years from now to think these were named from a bathing suit.

Admiral Lee: The target atoll was named Bikini. The bathing suit was named after the island, I believe, because the natives were very lightly clad - quite undressed. A lot of stories resulting from this little cruise that I talked about came out in the press. I don't know how the name Bikini as a garment came into being, but I suspect that these atom bomb test stories about Bikini and its natives might be the source.

Miss Kitchen: Then you went back for the second test. Were there any more incidents that you recall?

Admiral Lee: It was more of the same - the same difficulties. The press transmission had been improved to some degree. We got hundreds of letter of congratulations on how well things had been done, and I had many letters given to me by the correspondents saying they were grateful - the usual things that you get after these things - to indicate it wasn't nearly as bad as some people had portrayed it, but those don't make the press.

Miss Kitchen: But you did receive an official letter of commendation for your part in the operation.

Admiral Lee: Yes, I think I received a commendatory letter from SecNav. Actually Mr. Forrestal was out there for part of the tests and to my personal embarrassment, while he was giving a small talk to a group of officers and members of the press, the press got up and started praising the whole treatment of the press and the performance of the technical people who accomplished the difficult job of transmitting so much so fast, under bad conditions. I had the feeling that Mr. Forrestal would think that I had instigated the press to say these things because he knew he had had many complaints from press people in Washington. Since this wasn't true - I hadn't done any instigating - I was a little upset.

Miss Kitchen: I imagine his experience with the press, however, would let him know that they weren't going to say anything good unless they felt it.

Admiral Lee: If I could go back anecdotally for history - I would say that Mr. Forrestal's last days were marked by a great deal of unhappiness. He had a mental breakdown which, I think, was caused by a number of situations which I could not avoid being aware of since I was working right next door to his office and his personal aide was one of my closest friends. Mr. Forrestal's breakdown and suicide I personally attribute to two things. One was the fact that he was so strongly against Mr. Truman's policy of creating the state of Israel, but couldn't sway Mr. Truman. The second was the machinations of Mr. Drew Pearson in attacking Forrestal and putting out so many mis-truths about what he was doing and about what other good people in government were doing. Mr. Pearson was vehemently opposed to Mr. Forrestal and never hesitated to say something nasty about him whenever he could. Pearson made allegations about his personal family life, which was an unhappy one, and this had a great effect on Mr. Forrestal. It was entirely unnecessary.

In the spring of '48, I was selected to be a member of the class of the National War College. I prevailed upon Mr. Sullivan to let me go to that assignment which I might miss out on otherwise. He permitted me to go provided I could find another aide, which is the usual fate of people in these circumstances.

I spent a very delightful year at the War College. It was educational in many ways. I have always rhapsodized about the work of the National War College, which later on I headed for three years. Even in 1948 it was highly regarded even though it had only been in existence for three years. It is a unique institution and did a great deal to make the armed forces of the United States and the foreign service of the State Department do better work than they would have if the College hadn't existed. I am convinced of this, and I think ninety-eight percent of all the people who have had close relations with the War College are convinced of the same thing.

Here we were - a hundred students - our fourth Army, one fourth Navy and Marine, one fourth Air Force, and one fourth foreign service officers of the State Department and key civilians in other Executive Departments - thrown together for a year to examine every aspect of national security in relation to foreign policy. These students have access to the words and minds of people in top authority in Washington. An unbroken rule that has served the College well through all the years: That nothing that is said by any lecturer, or speaker, or participant in a seminar in the National War College will ever be attributed to him thereafter unless it is done with his permission. This means that people like the Secretary of State - even the President - can be subjected to probing questions on sensitive issues and can give straight answers. I can recall being astounded, while I was a student there, that very prominent people could and did say things on the platform even in very sensitive areas.

For me the principal asset of those years, and I think for all the War College students, was to get to know ninety-nine other people who had been selected to go there because they would probably be serving - and actually did serve - in positions of greater responsibility later on. You lived with them intimately for a year. From that moment on I was able to call friends of mine in the Air Force frequently in Washington or in other commands, and say, "Look, Bill, let's talk over this thing and get it straightened out." And it was straightened out. I could call people in the State Department and do the same thing, and vice versa. The fact that this college has had this seminal effect for some twenty-five years has been a remarkably good thing for the administration of government and foreign policy in the United States. I don't say that our policies have always been good, but I say they could have been much much worse if it hadn't been for the National War College.

I don't recall any particularly outstanding things other than my own impressions of these values that the War College was giving to us at that time. I went from the National War College to the job of Assistant Chief of Staff for Operations to Admiral Radford, who was then Commander-in-Chief of the Pacific Fleet and the Unified Pacific Command. The Korean War had just broken out.

Miss Kitchen: And you served there for two years.

Admiral Lee: Yes, serving for almost all of the Korean War. Yet my participation was, in spite of the the fact that I was Assistant Chief of Staff for Operations, really a sort of backwater office in some ways.

The tactical operations were all conducted in Korea under the command of the Commanding General of that Unified Command and under a United Nations aegis. Thus the staff operations of the Pacific Fleet were mostly in the logistic role of supplying the trained units that were sent to Korea, and replacing them as they needed replacement. This is basically what I did, and this is basically what Radford did. Nevertheless, he made frequent inspection trips out there and I would go with him, and we would be briefed on what was happening.

This sort of takes me again into the area in which I have been much concerned for all of my career - the organization of the Armed Forces of the United States - the unification battles, the roles and missions battles. We had examples of these things in Korea. The unification battles were a sort of underlying situation which affected the course of the war in some ways and dictated doing things which might not otherwise have been done, simply for the sake of proving a point by one service or another, as to what was good or what was bad from their point of view.

As an example, take the question of the close air support role, which has always been a major fight between the Army, and the Air Force, and the Navy, and the Marines. Usually the Army and Navy and Marines found themselves completely in agreement and opposed to the Air Force. The Air Force refused to give the Army what they wanted in the way of close air support; they want to do it the Air Force way, which is to have all the support aircraft under an Air Force commander who decides where the airplanes are needed. Over-simplifying, I could say the Army and Navy like the Marine type of organization where an air group is medded with a division of Marines. They work together as a team under the same commander all the time, one boss dictating how it should have been done, and with the ground commander being the top boss. The Army was

was the recipient of the Air Force support system, and the Marines weren't allowed to use their own system in Korea most of the time, but in some cases where the Army was working with Marine regiments and air groups it was obvious to the Army that the Marines on the ground were getting better tactical air support than their own Army divisions got from the Air Force units working with them, and they said so. This resulted in a great deal of correspondence and comment during and after the war, in which we were all somewhat involved.

Miss Kitchen: Was it ever resolved? Did they always have all different commands all during the Korean operation?

Admiral Lee: I don't think it has been resolved as of today, 1970.

I, of course, was involved in the discussions of this with the Army and Air Force officers on Radford's staff. Admiral Radford was CincPac, which was a Unified Command - all the Army, Navy, and Air Force under Radford. I was only on his Fleet staff, but we worked together with the Unified Staff in the same building.

However, all this from the point of view of unification came to a big roaring head when the B-36 controversy erupted. Admiral Radford, because of his great stature among the senior naval aviators, because he was a unified commander, and because he had occupied a strong position in the Navy as a highly respected spokesman for aviation for many years - for all these reasons - he became the naval spearhead for what was characterized in the press and elsewhere as "The Revolt of the Admirals."

Just to set the scene - the controversy stemmed from the fact that the Air Force had decided to build large numbers of the B-36, an intercontinental bomber. They were imbued, and had been since World War I, with the idea that the quickest and cheapest and most efficient and most humane way to win a war was to destroy the power and the will of the enemy to wage war. They said this could best be done by massive strategic air bombardment. As I mentioned earlier, this was preached by an Italian general named Douhet in 1917, and it was in the background thinking of all the top officers of SAC, the Strategic Air Command. They were in control of all the Air Force through these years.

The position of the Navy at the time the controversy broke was unhappy because naval aviation was being severely handicapped by cutting out air groups, cutting carriers out of commission (we were down to six carriers in commission by the time the Korean War started), and by the refusal to build the carrier UNITED STATES.

Meanwhile the Air Force had received funds for building the B-36 by short-circuiting the required procedures for the development of weapons. The rules required that the approval of the Joint Chiefs of Staff must be obtained before any weapons system was produced in quantity. This was all in writing ignoring these steps. The Air Force was building B-36s in large numbers, taking most of the money to do it. This matter came to a head in high places when accusations were made that this was wrong, and that the morale of the Navy was at a low ebb because of it. You may remember that Admiral Bogan wrote a letter to the Chief of Naval Operations which was leaked to the press and started the "revolt" of the admirals.

The House Armed Services Committee decreed that they would hold hearings on this subject, and the Navy had to get ready for its part in the hearing. The hearing was to be in two parts. One was concerned with the B-36 and the legality of the procedures being used and the validity of all the things being said about it. The Navy had said the B-36 couldn't do the job contemplated for it. The other was to be an examination of the part strategic bombing should play in national strategy. Admiral Radford became the leader of the team to present the Navy point of view at the second part of these hearings, and he was the lead-off spokesman. This was while he was still CincPac and CincPac Fleet.

Miss Kitchen: Were you with him at this time?

Admiral Lee: Yes, I was designated as his amanuensis and did most of the staff work for Admiral Radford's part in the hearings. So I spent a great deal of time going back and forth to

Washington, and working with Admiral Radford and others on his statement which was to be the framework for the Navy's presentations. Few of us knew the controversy was going to be as massive as it turned out to be.

Admiral Radford gave me the first outline of what he thought the Navy ought to say and I started writing drafts. I think the statement went through about twenty drafts. At each stage we would get in a bunch of people – from top admirals on down – and say, "Is this the right things?" We would refer parts of it back to Washington to get checked, and so forth. We worked for a long time on the statement, and I suppose I might be called the editor. I accompanied Admiral Radford, with some other people on our staff who had worked on it, to Washington for the hearings and stayed with him the whole time. It was a dramatic and traumatic experience for all of us in the Navy at that time. Admiral Radford's statement was the first statement to be made by a military person before the Armed Forces Committee in these hearings on national strategy.

The Secretary of the Navy was then Mr. Matthews, a banker who had just been appointed and who had little background knowledge of the Navy at the time. He was motivated, I think, very much by the feeling that he was sort of obligated to the President to keep the Navy under control and not let them go too far out. Mr. Matthews, whatever his other qualifications might be, was uneducated in military, national, and internation affairs – he was brought from a small mid-western banking situation and thrown into a maelstrom at this particularly important time. Revisions of Admiral Radford's statements were being made constantly almost up to the day before he was to present it. Mr. Matthews had never asked Radford to show him his statement. We were always afraid that he was going to, but he never did. Admiral Radford kept saying, "I am going up there to testify under oath, and these are my opinions and I must say them, even if Mr. Matthews wants me not to say them I probably will have to say them at a juncture like this, even though I am contravening the orders of my immediate superior."

The night before he was to appear before the hearings I was down in the Navy Department (then on Constitution Avenue) with a small secretarial staff to make the copies of the final draft. Mr. Matthews had never read any version of it. Nobody outside of the Navy Department had read it in its entirety, and we were in the process of cutting stencils and assembling the copies. I was called to the telephone about ten thirty at night and Mr. Matthews was on the line. He said, "I understand you have copies of Admiral Radford's statement." I said, "I have his statement, and we are now working on the reproduction of the copies to be used in Congress tomorrow." He said, "I would like you to bring me a copy." I said, "Mr. Matthews, I feel that I cannot do that unless I had Admiral Radford's permission to do so." And he said, "Well, get it."

I had difficulty locating Admiral Radford. He wasn't at his home, and I finally got him about a half an hour later. He said, "Let him have it." So then, after midnight I took the statement to Mr. Matthews' apartment hotel and gave it to him.

The next morning at the opening of the hearing, and after the preliminaries, Mr. Matthews got up and gave a brief statement of his own. Then he requested that the committee not permit Admiral Radford to give his statement in open session because he felt it was prejudicial to the best interest of the United States. The committee, Mr. Vinson was the chairman, said, "Well, we will read it and ask Admiral Radford to read it to us in executive session, and then we will determine whether we agree that this is all right to be given in open session." So Radford did read it in executive session, with only Radford in the chamber - nobody else - except the committee and no recording of it or anything.

Miss Kitchen: You were waiting outside?

Admiral Lee: Yes. This was done in the committee's private office. The big hearings were held in the main hearing room of the House Office Building, which seats maybe two hundred and fifty people, or three hundred people.

They came out and Vinson said, "We declare it's suitable for being read in public." So, great cheers among the press, and Admiral Radford read it in public. It had been designed to be read in public in the first place. I never have really understood why Mr. Matthews tried to keep it in executive session.

Admiral Radford was questioned for quite a long while. They talked about Bogan's statements, and the alleged low morale of the Navy, which was regretable because of the fact that morale means so many things to different people. When Admiral Bogan wrote that the morale of the Navy was low, he didn't mean that they weren't ready to go to war and fight to their best ability, but that the Navy was upset because it was being down-graded in appropriation to the degree that it couldn't do the job which it felt had to be done. It took many hours of the hearings to straighten out what morale meant, more or less, if it ever was straightened out.

Admiral Radford was asked at one stage, after saying that a lot of people in the Navy felt just as he did, Mr. Vinson asked him, "Who do you think agrees with you? Name some names." Admiral Radford started right off with Admiral King, Admiral Nimitz, every top admiral in the Navy. He had gone through about eight names, naming practically the whole leadership of the Navy, when Mr. Vinson said, "That's enough. We'll call them as witnesses," which he did. And the top of the Navy all testified in those hearings. They supported what Admiral Radford had said, to a man.

At the conclusion of the hearings the Committee published the entire hearings and later House Document 600 of the Eighty-first Congress, Second Session, on March 1, 1950. It is called "A Report of Investigation by the Committee on Armed Services, House of Representatives, on Unification and Strategy," which gave the Committee's conclusions. For anyone who is interested in unification and strategy per se, these documents provide a rich field of material; practically all aspects of them were covered and most of the material is still pertinent today.

As I look back from 1970, I can clearly recall why we were so vehement in our views and so emotionally tied up in the issues. They meant to us the existence or the failure to exist of the Navy, which had a long history of successful tradition and performance behind it and which we felt might be injured in such a way that it could never recover. Many statements were made by high officials to this effect, and equally strong statements were made by other high officials, some agreeing and some dissenting.

I well recall personally the testimony of General Bradley, who was then the Chairman of the Joint Chiefs of Staff. He normally has a rather high-pitched voice, but he got himself so worked up that toward the end he was talking in a voice so shrill you could scarcely make his words out. He was trembling. This was the talk in which he called the admirals a bunch of fancy Dans. It seemed incredible to me that an officer occupying the position that he held could become so emotional in such a circumstance.

Miss Kitchen: Do you feel Admiral Radford, in his presentation, was responsible for convincing the committee to reach the decision they did?

Admiral Lee: Yes, his and others. I think the final report of the committee vindicated the Navy. It was, and had to be, a semi-political document. It had to say things which didn't please the Navy in its entirety, and which we would argue with still, but in all we think that the basic issues were clearly set forth and the Navy position had been been upheld. This seems to have been the case through the years because the changes which we said should not be made have not been made. Although the hearts, and souls, and minds of many military men are still dedicated to what you might call parochial view points, there is a far greater understanding today and a far greater appreciation of the other fellow's role than had ever existed before. These are invaluable assets.

I am mindful now, in 1970, as we've just had another report of a presidentially appointed committee to investigate the Armed Forces, and the need for re-organization of the Pentagon. Many of the same issues are raised again by this committee. A very prominent industrialist of great aptitude was chosen to head the committee, a Mr. Fitzhugh. He, I'm sure, had a part in naming the other members of the committee. I am sure, from my knowledge of how committees like that are constituted in Washington, that once the decision was made to make an investigation and the chairman was named, there was a tremendous underground flurry to see who was going to be on the committee because that largely determines the decisions which will come out of it, and, more than that, who would be the working executive secretary and the working members of the staff of the committee, who probably would have as much or more influence than the members of the committee themselves. To my knowledge this has always been the case. I suppose, human nature being what it is, that's the way it always will be.

The same old things are being raked over again by the Fitzhugh Committee. They're asking for things which Mr. Symington was asking for in 1947, and again in 1960 when President Kennedy asked his views on re-organization of the Pentagon. I don't know, because I haven't read any detailed account of the hearings of the committee, but I could almost guarantee that Mr. Symington appeared before it and said the same things he said years ago, and others in the same vein. I don't think the Pentagon will be radically reorganized in accordance with the Fitzhugh Committee's recommendations. I could be wrong but if it is, it will be a departure from past precedents.

Miss Kitchen: When you were running off the copies of Admiral Radford's statement where were you?

Admiral Lee: I was in the private offices of the Secretary of the Navy in the old Navy Munitions Building on Constitution Avenue, where I had worked as the aide to the Secretary in past years. The reason it was done there was because I knew all the civil service staff in there and no place else was made available to me. So I went up and asked them if they would do it for me, and they did.

Miss Kitchen: Shall we go on to your next duty station?

Admiral Lee: I was detached from Admiral Radford's staff to take command of the carrier, FRANKLIN D. ROOSEVELT. I hated leaving the staff, but I had served two years and it was a normal rotation. I was glad to get command of a big ship, which is always the dream of most officers up until the time the dream comes true.

Miss Kitchen: Were you still a captain?

Admiral Lee: Yes. The ROOSEVELT was one of the three newest carriers at the time. It was a very fine ship and was in the Atlantic Fleet. I made a deployment to the Mediterranean for six months, and I had it for only thirteen months. The admiral on board with me as Commander Carrier Division Two was Admiral Pride, whom I liked a great deal and whom I knew very well. While we were in the Med his wife was there, and they did a good deal of entertaining on the ROOSEVELT for

Page 223 omitted by typist

local officials of the cities and ports that we went into, so we got to meet many of the prominent people in the ports around the Mediterranean and in Portugal. The Prides always used me because I had gone to school in France and had spent three years in Latin America so I could speak fairly fluent, although fractured, French and Spanish and this was useful in that area. Many times when I didn't particularly want to go I went as an interpreter nevertheless.

We were performing the conventional, so to speak, duties of the principal carrier of the Sixth Fleet in the Mediterranean. The Sixth Fleet commander at that time was Admiral Garnder. He and I were good friends. He used to like to send rather short terse messages bawling out his ship captains whenever he found an opportunity. I got my share, and used to go over and talk them over and try to straighten them out.

I also saw a great deal of the NATO navies. We had many exercises with them. I had had very little of that before and it was interesting to me. I was impressed with some of their great assets and some of their tremendous handicaps. I was also impressed with the fact that in many instances some of the Navy crews of other nations seemed to be better educated as a whole and their ships better run in some respects than ours were, particularly the British who had a very fine professional educational system - the officers, mostly, and their ships were extremely smart, too. They had many career enlisted men who were in their fourteenth or sixteenth years of naval service. The average years of experience as a sailor on a British was maybe eight or ten years, whereas ours was probably eight or ten months. This was true also of the French, and the Turkish, and the Greek navies. They were limited but they had some things which were good things to have and which we lacked.

Miss Kitchen: It's wonderful to get that view and not think that we tend to be somewhat conceited as to our own competence.

Admiral Lee: I think this was one of the things that impressed me a great deal and got me more involved, more than I had been in the past, I think, with the subject of morale and leadership, and how morale depends on good treatment of the sailors. To make them have the feeling that they want to re-enlist you've got to make a way of life for them that they like. Many of our people didn't have it then, and don't have today. This is one of the greatest handicaps we have today. These were brought home to me by close association with some of the NATO navies, who were grossly inferior to us in many technical ways.

I also had some time to renew my reading of naval history and the history of the Mediterranean area. I've always been interested in history. We published a little ship's newspaper. Before we went into each port I required that the paper have a history of the country, its naval heritage, all the big things that had happened there through the centuries, and to relate this to its naval accomplishments and world history. I found myself to be ending up writing most of these things.

Miss Kitchen: Do you know whether this writing of history had been done before for other ships, Admiral?

Admiral Lee: Oh, I'm sure it was in one way or another. As a matter of fact, I read many things like that that other people had written in spotty ways. I had a friend in the French Navy and he had done that for French ships and I had read some of his things. But I didn't have them with me on the ROOSEVELT, and I had to rely on what routine texts were available, and they weren't very rich in their background. But they made interesting reading and the crew liked them, and it did awaken an appreciation I think in the ship, which was valuable.

Miss Kitchen: I think it would have been tragic for them to have gone ashore in a foreign country without haveing any recognition of the kind of nation it was, the people they were going to meet.

Admiral Lee: I don't want to imply that I was doing something entirely innovative here which had never been done before; it had been. The thing was that you need to renew, and for the benefit of newcomers to the ship, these things. I think this aspect frequently slipped. A ship that's been in the Fleet over there has made two cruises to the Sixth Fleet, still has a modicum of the same people on board, and the old hands aboard forget that in the interim they've gotten about sixty percent new people on board and it's strange to them. They are disinclined to rehash the whole thing over again in the ship's paper. Small ships that haven't got much background material to work with often have very little other than a tourist brochure that you pick up in a travel agency.

Miss Kitchen: I think you said you put these together and recommended to the Navy Department that they be issued to all ships in the Sixth Fleet.

Admiral Lee: I did. I think they went via CincLant Fleet, and I never heard of them anymore. I don't know where they are, if there are any. It was interesting at the time because it did make me do a lot of reading again, and educated me better.

Miss Kitchen: In our present educational system how many people would have been aware of what they were seeing if you hadn't done it for them?

Admiral Lee: Very few, because I was pinning most of this to naval tradition, to the influence of sea power in the development of the Mediterranean nations, which, of course, was very considerable.

I was always very interested in the subject of morale and leadership and I tried to put a lot of techniques, so to speak, to work. Sometimes I doubted that they did work, but some of them may have done pretty well. On the F.D.R. we always made a practice, I think I have mentioned it before in this oral history, of having a person describe what was going on to the crew when things of interest were happening.

We had a lot of division parties ashore. When invited I always went to and stayed, I hoped, just the right length of time, just to show the people that I had an interest in the fact that they were having one. I saw many strange dives and funny little restaurants that I never would have heard of as a result of some of those little interludes.

I felt that the dedication of the officers for the men under them was the thing that was of greatest importance, and I worked hard on all the division officers. I tried to make them feel that they were the linchpins of the whole organization, as they are, and I think I made some dents in that on the ROOSEVELT. Anyway, I think we had a pretty happy ship.

We had lots of little gimmicks, you might call them. We had a helicopter, which was the ship's rescue helicopter, and we named it Fala, which was President Roosevelt's black Scottish terrier in the White House days. He was quite renowned as a dog, so we had Fala painted in large letters on the side of our helicopter, which got us into some trouble.

I think the trouble ended up as a morale advantage, but some of the authoritites didn't care for this nick-naming of the helicopter. No other helicopters had nicknames on them, so this became a minor issue, but I said it was a big morale builder and it was fine. Then somebody said it would probably make the Roosevelt family unhappy, so I wrote back to Mrs. Roosevelt, for whom I had worked in the White House years ago. I sent her some pictures and said, "I'm having some troubles keeping Fala in commission here. I need to know if you have any objections so I can remove that as a possible objection." She had another picture taken of the picture and autographed it, "To your Fala from the owner of the last one," which once hung in the CPO mess, I think, on the ROOSEVELT.

From the ROOSEVELT I was transferred to duty as the Commanding Officer of the Naval Air Station at Norfolk and as Commander Naval Air Bases, Fifth Naval District. The later is the principal title, but the former is the tail that wags the dog. A large percentage of my time was taken with running the Naval Air Sation, which was the biggest in the United States at the time, and probably shares with the Naval Air Station at San Diego the same distinction today. It was my first experience with civil service en masse. In those years an air station job tended to be given to an officer who hadn't made out well in getting a good command at sea. So assignment to command of a big air station was sort of looked upon as a sop, but marked you as being somebody who wouldn't go very far after that. This was just an attitude — maybe it didn't have much basis in fact, but it was the feeling among my contemporaries at least. So when I heard I was being sent to command an air station I was unhappy about it. The person who did the detailing said that this a new policy, that they felt that with all the things that went on ashore in the Navy, which many of the tops of the Navy didn't know much about until faced with them in later years and needed to be educated about it at that stage, it wasn't a good system. So they were going to insist on putting people with a future ahead of them in command of the big stations on one tour of duty so they would get that education.

Well, I didn't think it was a good idea at the time, but after I finished my time at Norfolk I strongly concurred. It was a new life in a way because Norfolk had a large airplane overhaul facility there and employed some eight thousand civilian employees. I would say at least half of my time was concerned with civil service problems in that station — labor problems and community relations incident to that aspect. The military part of running the air station just took care of itself, but the rest of it dealt with things which I was naive about and I learned at my own pain and penury. For this reason I got into several arguments with Mr. Drew Pearson, who still didn't like me.

Miss Kitchen: How did that happen?

Admiral Lee: I think I made the Drew Pearson column three times as a named individual (two of them in that tour) and I've always lost the argument, although I was right according to me. One of these was a Pearson story that a Navy airplane had taken off and crashed shortly after take-off. The subsequent investigation had proved that a wrench had been dropped into the sump of one of the engines, which had been overhauled at the Naval Air Station at Norfolk, commanded by Captain Fitzhugh Lee, and that this was the way they ran Navy air stations, and this was the reason for the great loss of life, and probably nothing would be done to punish him. Well, nothing was done to punish me other than my publicity in the Drew Pearson column. I had made the mistake of trying to argue with him about his alleged facts, and his inferences that the Navy wasn't concerned for the safety of their people.

Miss Kitchen: How had he gotten that story?

Admiral Lee: Somebody writes it to him. Maybe it's a mechanic writes to his wife and says, "We found a wrench in the thing," and she writes to Drew Pearson and says my husband's brother was lost in this and this is the way the Navy does. In that actual incident it wasn't a wrench; it was a tiny little bolt that had dropped in and it was one of those things that can happen once in a while in spite of rigorous inspection procedures. But he indicated the whole overhaul and repair organization of the Naval Air Station, which had done magnificent work over the years, although it had never been patted on the back for it by Pearson. But when he found a little thing like that he excoriated the whole system. I was trying to get him to publish something, or the local Norfolk paper who had printed the Pearson column, to correct it or to publish something that would put another side to it. We couldn't do either. That's the way it goes.

An interesting aspect of that year, or so, in command of the air station was also the fact that of our eight thousand employees a substantial number were Negroes — about twenty-five or thirty percent. It was about this time that Mr. Truman, followed by President Eisenhower, put out the order that all vestiges of segregation in the armed forces would be abandoned, period. This was quite a problem for air stations and other military installations in the southern part of the United States, where things were done according to the custom of the country, so to speak. For as long as anyone could remember Norfolk had separate rest room facilities for the Negroes, and a separate restaurant for the Negroes. I thought this was all wrong, myself, but it was the custom and the great mass of the local people, the community from which all these people came, felt that this was the way of life, and for the military to change their way of life right in their midst was something that they resented a great deal.

A day was named when all these things had to be completely changed. The black and whites were all to use the same restaurants, rest rooms, and so forth. When the day came it all worked well with only minor problems, but the anticipation of the problem was quite a Gethsemane, so to speak. Everything was going to happen — we were going to have riots; people were going to march; this, that, and the other thing. I just kept saying, " Well, it's going to be this way and this is the way we have to do it." However, many of my top civil servants, white people (these were the principal people that caused the problem) were very adamant that I should take strong steps to resist, to request delays, to do it more gradually. I just had to say no to all of it, which I think was the only sensible thing to do. But it caused a great deal of resentment among the top white civil servant people at the station.

Miss Kitchen: Did you have any preparatory meetings between blacks and whites?

Admiral Lee: Oh yes, we went through a long educational process to get it all squared away and we had no incidents of any worthwhile sort.

Miss Kitchen: Were there any top black leaders that helped you work out the problem?

Admiral Lee: In retrospect, and with faulty memory, I cannot recall any of the employees, any of the black employees, in a leadership capacity coming up to us. We did talk to several black people who were fairly high up in their own hierarchy; we aked them to come in and talk to us. They didn't furnish any information that was very workable or offer any suggestions. They were glad to see it happen, I think, but didn't want to appear too happy to say so. A local NAACP man came down from Richmond and asked if there were going to be any problems. We told him there wouldn't be, not knowing if there would be or not.

Miss Kitchen: None of the dire predictions came true?

Admiral Lee: No, but it was an interesting experience. That and other community relations factors were interesting educational things to me.

The end of the Norfolk runway, the only principally used runway, ended at a little narrow creek, and on the other side of it was a close packed civilian housing development, filled with homes and children. Night flying always resulted in a rash of complaints from the neighborhood about the noise - "My baby's sick," "You're ruining this and that," "I'm sending my wife to a sanatarium," and that kind of thing. Some of it sometimes got rather vicious. They would call me, the Commanding Officer, at ten or twelve at night. We had one particularly anonymous caller who was real stinky in his attitude and voice, and choice of words. He would call various people, sometimes in the day, sometimes at night. We couldn't find out who this person was. He wouldn't give his name, and there weren't any means that the telephone company had of identifying him. We finally discovered him through some neighborhood talk and identified him. He turned out to be a U. S. naval aviator on active duty. So that was a lesson of sorts in human nature to me. He didn't happen to be working for the Naval Air Station, but he was attached to a squadron that was based there.

Miss Kitchen: When was the second time you made Pearson's column?

Admiral Lee: The second time was in connection with two aviation pilots, enlisted pilots. We had quite a number of them at that time. They took one of our Naval Air Station planes up to Willow Grove, Pennsylvania, to get some cargo and it wasn't ready when they got there. So they ended up by sitting in a little coffee shop just outside the Willow Grove air station gate drinking beer, and they got pretty high. They came back and got in their airplane and started to taxi out before the tower people were aware that they were tipsy. They were the only two people in the airplane, no mechanic, it was just a cargo plane. The tower operator finally persuaded them to turn around instead of taking off, and to come back. While coming in, they taxied into two other airplanes and caused damage to all three - their own and the two others.

This incident didn't make the newspapers anywhere up at Willow Grove, and it didn't make the newspapers anywhere in Norfolk. It wasn't a major incident; it was regrettable, improper, and everything was wrong about it, but there was no terrific harm done.

Miss Kitchen: It wasn't an indictment of naval aviation.

Admiral Lee: No. It wasn't a thing that you'd want necessarily to send down to the papers to say we had this incident occur, please print it, and we hadn't.

The two chiefs were tried by general court martial, and in connection with this general court martial their civilian lawyers brought out that all this had happened. They, or somebody, as a result of being in the court room, gave it to Drew Pearson, who then accused me of taking deliberate steps to keep this secret. I said we hadn't tried to do that, an then I got into more problems. I also had made a mistake, which caused unhappy consequences. One of the pilots was a fellow I had known for years, and I talked to him before we ordered the general court martial. I said, "This is the silliest thing I think you and your buddy are wrong in pleading not guilty in a thing like this. It may lead to a situation which will end up worse for you, I'm sure. There are so many witnesses that are going to say what happened, and you know what happened."

He had come to my office on his own and asked my advice, and he admitted at the time they had just sat there and had too much to drink and hadn't realized it. But he didn't take my advice and in the trial he swore that he had not had anything to drink. They got the proprietor of the bar down from Willow Grove to swear that there were a lot of people there and he couldn't tell whether the men were drinking ice tea or beer. The civilian lawyers had made a big case of the fact that I had told a man under my command to plead not guilty when this was an improper thing for me to do. I just didn't realize at the moment that it was improper. I thought I was helping the guy, but I wasn't, and I acted illegally. Pearson made the most of it.

Miss Kitchen: Fortunately you had good experiences with the major part of the press.

Admiral Lee: I'm still interested in the press and national security. I think the press and the armed forces have a lot more to do in working better together. I don't hold much hope.

My jobs as the skipper and Chief of Naval Air Bases were routine in most respects. They were educational for me and I enjoyed the duty and am glad I had it. I also learned a little bit more about the workings of Congress because I became mindful of the extreme interest that the local congressmen take in the federal civil servants in their districts. I tilted windmills in that area in one case.

We had a painter who suffered from paint poisoning so he couldn't be allowed to paint, but under civil service rules you had to give him a job. He wasn't a very good worker anyway. Here he was, hired as a painter but not allowed to paint because of his physical problems with paint. So we wanted either to make him change his rate and learn a new trade and be hired again, or quit. We found we couldn't do either one. I got my best windmill tilting lance all sharpened up and said, "I shall see this through to the end." Well, I did, and it ended up in a hearing before the top three of the Civil Service Commission in Washington. The case went all the way up to the top, and we lost. We had to keep on hiring him, and couldn't let him paint.

Miss Kitchen: You paid him for doing nothing?

Admiral Lee: No, we gave him jobs to do but they weren't in his rate, and they prevented other people in that rate from doing the job. The top man, who has just recently retired as chairman of the Civil Service Commission, was the one who made the decision.

Miss Kitchen: Shall we leave that interesting assignment, and go on?

Admiral Lee: I became COMCARDIV Fourteen, an anti-submarine carrier group - an aircraft carrier with eight destroyers and a target submarine to work with it. We were one of the hunter-killer groups of the Atlantic Fleet.

I made another cruise to the Mediterranean in my flag ship, which was then the ANTIETAM. We also had some interesting experiences in cold weather operations. We were sent up into the Davis Strait between Greenland and Canada for cold weather tests. We also had a visit to Halifax in connection with Canadian Navy Day.

I didn't mention it but one of the dividends of the National War College, when I went to it as a student, was that there were three officers of the Canadian armed forces and three officers of the United Kingdom armed forces - Army, Navy, and Air Force - who were students by special arrangement. Our class in 1949 was the last class to have these Britishers, which was regrettable because we were so close to the British and Canadians that it could mutually be very helpful.

With the establishment of NATO, and with Canada, Britain, and the United States all being members of NATO, other NATO nations applied to have students at the National War College in the United States. If we acceeded we would have had to take students from countries we distrusted, because their armed forces had known security leaks and members of the Communist Party in them. Also we were ignorant about what kinds of people we would get among the Portuguese, Turks, and Greeks, as to their backgrounds and loyalties.

In the end we decided we had to limit students to American Nationals and that's the way it still stands. This comes to mind because of the fact that one of the head men in Halifax was a very close friend of mine. He later became the Chief of Naval Operations of the Canadian Navy. He was a Canadian officer who was a classmate at the National War College, and I had gotten to know very well at that time.

Miss Kitchen: You had that job from November '53 to March '55, and then went out to Commander Fleet Air Japan and Commander Naval Air Bases Japan.

Admiral Lee: And also Commander Fleet Air Western Pacific. I had three titles.

Miss Kitchen: You were out in the Western Pacific for two full years?

Admiral Lee: Yes, I was headquartered at the Naval Air Station at Atsugi, Japan. My job was as Commanding Officer of the air station there. I was also the boss of all the other naval air stations which we had in Japan. They varied in number in that period, but there were three or four then. I was also Commander Fleet Air Western Pacific, which meant that everything from Australia to Saghalien, if it had anything to do with U. S. naval aviation, was in my province, or under my technical aeronautical supervision. These included the Naval Air Stations at Cubi Point and Sangley Point in the Philippines, the Naval Air Bases on Okinawa, the naval air activities in Korea, and so on.

Miss Kitchen: Would you identify the location of Saghalien?

Admiral Lee: Yes, Saghalien is an island just off the coast of Siberia and north of Japan. The southern half of it was captured from Russia in the Russo-Japanese War in 1905, and was restored at the end of World War II. I believe Mr. Roosevelt and Mr. Hiss and some others promised at Yalta to give it back to Russia. This was long before the war was ended. It's now all Russian.

Our two years in Japan were wonderful for the Lees. I had my wife and children there. Our boys were about six and seven. We traveled a good deal in Japan as a family, and I traveled all over the Western Pacific quite frequently. I went to various places as a tourist and as a government official. These were pleasant years. Our relations with the Japanese were basically good and our relations with the U. S. Air Force out there were good too. I'd had the background, which I've previously mentioned, of a lot of experience in Japan many years before, and a little appreciation of Japanese culture. This made it easier for me to talk with the Japanese military officers, naval officers, all of whom talked with the greatest of frankness about their experiences in the war.

Miss Kitchen: Did you ever meet anyone who had been in any of the operation or engagements that you had been?

Admiral Lee: Generally not, in any meaningful relationship. The Japanese naval officers on active duty in the Japanese Navy, in the years when I was there in the mid fifties, were mostly younger officers during World War II; they hadn't been in jobs of great responsibility, or in planning or in sensitive positions. All the people with that kind of background had been forced out. Not only that, they were forced out with no retirement pensions, no nothing - they were paupers. I met a number of those.

I think I mentioned earlier of coming back to Japan in later years and seeking out my old friend from Washington days and finding him. He was a little vegetable gardenfarmer, livin by the work of his hands, digging up and planting potatoes and rice and selling it, and just barely able to make a living for the rest of his life. He was typical of almost all of them I talked to and heard about many others in his same straits.

I also met some of their leading characters - General Genda I met quite often. He was a vocal and able Japanese officer who was able to continue in the Japanese Air Force. He was a naval officer who came into the independent Air Force when it was created after the war. He was a naval aviator and had written a widely read book, and was on the operations' staff of Yamashita in the war and in the Battle of Midway.

My memory may be poor about the foregoing, anyway he was a dynamic, able man. He caused quite a stir in fairly recent years when he came to America and spoke to the midshipmen at the Naval Academy and to the Naval War College in Newport, Rhode Island. There was a lot of caustic comment in the press about the propriety of this. Anyway, I had many contacts with the Japanese and enjoyed them.

The Japanese were always extremely frank in their statements, their openness about the whole thing - their realization which I felt was frank and sincere, that they had adopted a course in the late thirties which they felt wasn't best for the nation - that they should have taken another course of action.

One of my friends whom I got to know fairly well was Admiral Nomura, who was sent to Washington to plead the case of Japan for the scrap iron and other materials just before Pearl Harbor was about to be attacked. He knew nothing about the impending Pearl Harbor, and yet was sent as an emissary even though his government knew that they were going to attack Pearl Harbor when he would be in Washington. Nomura was greatly upset by this bit of trickery, which he did not know about in advance. He was a wonderful old man, and his daughter was a very attractive person. They came to our house several times, and he was full of interesting anecdotes and observations. If historians want to know more about him, he was a close friend and admirer of Admiral Burke, and I'm sure Admiral Burke must have written much about him.

We had interesting things happening all the time, it seemed to me. One that made a great impression one me about the culture of the Japanese - which one has to admire if you get to know it really: the fact that they lived for eight hundred years almost completely isolated from the rest of civilization and developed a way of life, a system of ethics and philosophics entirely different from ours. These things seem strange to us at first, and then when we get to know them better, we sometimes began to wonder if perhaps they didn't have a better view point than we did.

An incident which stems in part from this comes to my mind. The U. S. Air Force had a big field at Tachikawa, about forty miles north of Atsugi. They wanted to lengthen a runway of the field to make it useable for larger planes. This stirred up a tremendous fuss because it involved condemning many peasant homes and land holdings which would have to be plowed under, in order to extend the air-strip. It became a highly emotional issue with the Japanese at a time when our mutual Security Treaty with the Japanese was coming up for renewal. Many small incidents occurred which normally would cause little difficulty, but would be magnified by the Japanese press and the students.

Anyway, the lengthening of the Tachikawa Air Field became a major issue. Large demonstrations and riots took place in several cities in Japan, but finally the Japanese government went in and started bulldozing the homes even though the families would not get out of them. They would bulldoze a whole flimsy house and barn with the people and animals in them. One of the Japanese farmers was asked by a member of the press why he felt so strongly about this land because he only held a tiny piece - about the size of one floor of a large American home. He said, "I am the only member of my family, bearing my family's surname, who is left with land holdings in this area and I have to keep them because they have been in my family for one thousand and seven years."

Another incident comes to mind which I've never seen publicized in the United States, although I've often told the story. At the close of the war, when I was on CincPac's, Admiral Nimitz's staff in Guam, I went up to the Bonin Islands between Japan and Guam. The Japanese garrison there had shortly beforehand surrendered. We were adapting some of their installations to serve as communications stations. The American officer in charge said, "I'd like to show you something of interest." He took me up to a thickly-wooded canyon to an enormous, oblong, concrete, building in the jungle. It was all finished and was about the size of a tennis court with a cover over it about forty feet high. Alongside it was another similar building, which was only about half finished. The interior was lined completely with copper, heavy gauge copper, and there was a machinery room in which air conditioning machinery had been installed, and a small administrative office in the building but outside of the inner copper shell. The copper shell had one opening into it, through a big heavy door which looked like a bank vault. The building was empty when we took over, but the story about it was handed down by the people there, and I believe it is true.

The Japanese have an intensely strong consciousness of their national treasures and art objects. They constitute the national treasures. Each one is carefully labeled, numbered, registered, documented, and so forth. Even if they remain in private ownership, as is the case often, they have regulations covering their care. They can't be sold, and the government monitors their care. Many of them are several thousand years old, and are very beautiful things - some are tiny vases an inch or two high and some are hugh statues of carved wood.

This vault was built in the Bonin Islands to serve as a place where the Japanese could put many of the national treasures when the expected invasion of the Japanese Islands took place. It was in a very inaccessible ravine and they had extensively camouflaged it. You would never know that anyting was there. The Bonins themselves are isolated and little visited. This was the place where many of the Japanese treasures were to go. It was quite a remarkable spot.

In my later years in Japan I asked several Japanese about this. I never found one who had heard about it, but many agreed that it was logical and probably true. I can't conceive of any other reason for these casemates being in the Bonins. They were never used; they never got to the point of putting anything in them, but I'm sure it was their plan to put their treasures there.

I recall that Chiang Kai Shek took most of the most prized art treasures of China to Formosa.

I had consideralbe to do with the build-up of Japan's naval aivation forces. They were rudimentary in the extreme, as was their navy as a whole in those years. Admiral Nagasawa was the Chief of Naval Operations. I looked on him as a good friend and our relationships were frequent and pleasant. He was always seeking my advice and that of other officers of the American Navy in Japan at the time. Knowing him was a pleasure. He took me around to many interesting places I'd never been to in Japan. I visited the Japanese Naval Academy in his company. I had seen it when I had been in Japan before, but I had only been allowed to view the outside as a tourist. This time I was taken all through the whole plant. Oddly enough, some of the buildings were patterned somewhat after the Naval Academy at Annapolis and after Dartmouth in England. Admiral Togo's tomb is there and encased is his ashes. It is a big block of black marble. There is a little cubby hole in the top with a marble lid on it. Inside is a little wooden box containing some of the hair, fingernails, and toenails of Admiral Togo. This is a thing the Japanese do in their burial customs, because the hair and the fingernails and toenails continue to grow for a considerable time after the body is dead.

I also went to Hiroshima and Nagasaki in those years, and saw what the Japanese had done to memorilize the atomic bomb. It is considerable, and sort of soul shaking.

By our standards the Japanese are very frank in many ways and very modest in others. It's always a strange contrast. Community bathing is the usual custom and they have mixed male and female bathing in all the bath houses in Japan. But you will never see a naked figure in Japanese art, male or female, anywhere - they are always clothed. Our modern, classic, undressed Greek nudes, they think are indecent. In one of the principal museums in Kamakura, where the big Buddha is, there is an exhibit of the birth of a baby, all in glass jars from sperm to baby, which is visited by thousands of school children all year long.

In Hiroshima they have a museum of the atom bomb blast. In it, preserved in glass jars for all the people to see, are specimens of human flesh injured one way or another as a result of the bomb, including the progressive deterioration due to radiation, plus hundreds of photographs at their grizzliest. At the center of a large devasted area in the middle of town (which they've left devasted) they have put a big sort of ogival arch. Underneath it is a little rock with a plate saying, "This was ground zero when the bomb was dropped." The museum is quite extensive. It was interesting, while spending a day there, to see all the little children playing around, using the area as a playground, flying model airplanes, everybody going to the little arch marking ground zero. In Japan, which is a nation of tourists, everybody has to have a tourist souvenir book in which is placed a rubber stamp called a "chop" which says, "I visited this historic beauty spot." There were lines of as many as a hundred and fifty people waiting to get their "chop" under the ground zero arch at Hiroshima.

As Commander Fleet Air Western Pacific I also traveled a good deal in Okinawa and the Philippines and Korea. This was interesting and educational, meeting the people - Chiang Kai-Shek, Madam Chiang, Syngman Rhee in Korea, talking with him and with the president of the Philippines, Magsaysay, who was subsequently killed - one of the greatest tragedies for the Philippines, I think, because he was a man of real vision who might have done so much. None of his successors have been able to fill his boots.

I was continually impressed in these years with the evidence of the extraordinary industry, imagination, and determination of the Japanese in their preparations for war - World War II. I only saw the vestiges - this was about ten years after the war - but I hadn't seen them when I was a tourist visitor in the thirties. I hadn't been allowed to see them. Several of them come to mind.

Atsugi was a Japanese airfield which had under it several miles of underground passageways and innumerable caves. They had a complete aircraft engine overhaul and assembly plant underground at Atsugi. The earth there is very soft and the digging is easy. They had intended living in the caves, and had all the facilities for it.

This was true all over Japan. You saw these tremendous cave complexes where they had everything underground to protect them from American bombing and from what they expected would be the final invasion of Japan. They were determined to defend it to the last Japanese - there's no question about it.

Another one was the tremendous oil storage complex on an island near Sasebo. They had taken an island, dug a tremendous big hole in the ground, and made a big compartmented oil tank. I've forgotten the number of millions of gallons that it held, but it was like taking two or three city blocks, digging down to about eighty feet and then making this hugh tank, then covering it all over, and then restoring the whole island to look like it was before. It practically occupied the whole island. Cruising by it in a boat you would never know that it was there - just a few little docks around the edges and things of that sort. I think it must undoubtedly be the biggest oil tank in the world, before or since. We never knew about it until after the war, so we never bombed it.

Miss Kitchen: No pictures or reconnaisance.

Admiral Lee: No. It makes me sometimes wonder about our great belief in aerial surveillance of installations in Russia these days. I'm convinced that as wonderful as is the photography from satellites and airplanes, it certainly has its limitations.

I could point to that oil tank that I don't think any U-2, or any modern development, would reveal. And this was true of many, many installations in Japan – huge big underground centers of activity, operational centers, communications industries, hospitals – all underground.

Miss Kitchen: That's been proven in Vietnam as well.

Admiral Lee: Yes. This was one of my big impressions of post-war Japan – the efforts they made, especially the underground efforts, which we knew really nothing about. We saw evidences of it in the various places we captured as the Pacific war progressed, but we had no idea of the magnitude of it in the homeland of Japan.

I had also occasion to talk to many people in Japan about our Strategic Bombing Survey. This was made at the end of World War II, first in Europe and subsequently in the Pacific. It was an investigation to determine the value of strategic bombing. The Air Force had encouraged and, I think, sponsored it to begin with, with the idea that it would prove that strategic bombing, the Douhet theory, was correct. In Germany it didn't quite turn out the way the Air Force wanted it to go. There were many things in the survey which led to the belief that there were some gaps in Douhet.

I'm not sure of this, but I think there was some opposition on the part of the Air Force to have a Strategic Bombing Survey of Japan made at all. Anyway one was made, and there was a large task force involved in it. Some close friends of mine - Rear Admiral Ofstie, Captain James S. Russell (subsequently Admiral Russell), and Commander Thomas Moorer (subsequently Chairman of the Joint Chiefs of Staff) - were members of this commission.

While I was still on Nimitz's staff at the end of the war I got involved in this, not directly, but professionally interested in their work. In my subsequent work in Washington I profited from this, in connection with some of the unification hearings. It is these that I would like to mention now.

The titular head of the Pacific Strategic Bombing Survey was a Mr. D'Olier, long time head of the Prudential Insurance Company of America. The number two, and executive director for the Pacific part of it was Paul Nitze, who subsequently became the Secretary of the Navy, and Under SecDef, and held other big jobs in government. Ofstie was the head of the Navy section of the Strategic Bombing Survey of Japan. There were many sub-task forces, each looking into the results of our strategic and tactical operations in the war. Moorer and Russell were two of his many assistants. There was a corresponding group of Air Corps people working on the analysis of Army Air Corps operations. These studies and many others became the Strategic Bombing Survey of the war in the Pacific.

There was a principal text plus conclusions and recommendations which were signed by Mr. D'Olier and other people including, I think, Mr. Nitze. This was the official version of what went on. There were also about fifty appendices, written by the various task forces studying the petroleum industry, the steel industry, communications, this and that phase of the war. One appendix was called, "Naval Air Campaigns in the Pacific," which was written by Ofstie and his task force after they had inspected the damage and interviewed many Japanese leaders in order to assess what had happened in various air campaigns against the Japanese - not just from our point of view, but also from the Japanese point of view as to what we had done which contributed to their defeat.

The Air Corps had made comparable studies, but they had not produced anything called, "Air Corps Campaigns of the Pacific," as an appendix to the basic report. All the appendices were a part of the official record of the report, and had to be approved by Mr. D'Olier as such. "The Naval Air Campaigns of the Pacific" reenforced our statements about the effectiveness of naval aviation in its contest with Japanese aviation in sinking ships and things of that sort, and included the testimony of the Japanese. The Air Corps had been so obsessed with the subject of the actual bombing of Japan that they hadn't bothered very much with these other aspects of air power in the Pacific War, and there was no separate appendix marked, "Air Corps Campaigns of the Pacific."

After the Survey people returned to Washington and the Report was in its final draft form, some of the Air Corps people came to the conclusion that they ought to write something about the Air Corps campaign in the Pacific to contravene the propaganda that the Navy was supposed to have placed in theirs, and which had been documented and approved for publication. Well, they quickly put together an "Air Corps Campaigns in the Pacific War," which wasn't as well documented and was apparently simply aimed at refuting the Navy report, as well as to give another side of the picture as the Air Corps saw it. It was outspoken and concluded that the data proved that there had to be only one Air Force and no Naval Aviation. It gave many statistics which we thought wrong or unfounded; in fact it seemed to be carelessly put together and malicious in that it was mostly a diatribe aimed at the Navy. Whereas we had merely recounted what the Navy had done and the lessons thereby learned, the Air Corps was saying what the Navy did and why it was wrong, or things of that sort. I don't know the details now, but that was the general attitude of the Air Corps approach in their document.

Admiral Ofstie didn't know anything about the Air Corps document until it was almost finished and ready for the printer. By established procedure he should have seen it much earlier and it should have had an official okay from several people as well before it was even undertaken as an official appendix of the Strategic Bombing Survey. Ofstie thought that the whole thing was improper regardless of its content and that it should not be included in the final report. He had several arguments with the content also. An internicine battle ensued and while it was still going on the Air Corps document was printed in exactly the same format as the other appendices.

Admiral Ofstie wrote in protest to Mr. Nitze and to Admiral Sherman, then CNO. Mr. Nitze replied that he was sorry it had been printed and was going to be included in the report. He had been short-circuited and Mr. D'Olier had made the decision; Nitze hadn't even known about it. And there was more to come.

When the final Report reached the White House and before it was published, Mr. Truman sent it back to Mr. D'Olier because the basic report failed to make the recommendation that a single independent U. S. Air Force was demonstrated to be necessary as a result of the lessons of the Pacific War. We didn't think it did. Moreover the Strategic Bombing Survey Committee hadn't reached that conclusion. Mr. Truman directed that such a conclusion be made, so Mr. D'Olier revised the report to show what the President wanted. After that Mr. Truman signed it. A great many copies were printed and are now on the shelves of libraries all over the world. The Table of Contents lists only fifty appendices. The Air Corps document "Air Corps Campaigns of the Pacific War," was attached and numbered #51.

We thought all this was dishonest. Mr. D'Olier died a year or two later. We never knew who influenced the President. I don't know if this had any great bearing on the establishment of the separate Air Force in the National Security Act of 1947. I don't recall that this incident came up in any of the hearings before the Act was adopted.

2 Lee - 256

Miss Kitchen: Anyone looking at this report might look only at the conclusion that if they didn't know there were maneuverings by which the report, in fact, became published, they would reach an improper conclusion, I would suggest.

Admiral Lee: To the best of my knowlege no official statement has been made by anybody in authority indicating that the Strategic Bombing Survey had not found this to be a conclusion, but that the Survey was forced to say that it was a conclusion by direction of the White House.

Miss Kitchen: I should think anyone going into the full problem would find this valuable.

Admiral Lee: After my duty as ComFairWesPac I was assigned, without returning to the United States, to duty as Commander Carrier Division Five, which was one of the Pacific Fleet carrier divisions. I had that job for a year. About six months of it was in the Western Pacific, from which my family had gone home. Then I came back and was based in San Diego for the last six months.

My first six months in the Western Pacific was fairly routine. There were none of the major confrontations which occurred and in which the Carrier Division Commander would be much concerned if the cookie happened to crumble in a certain way. As Commander Carrier Division Five, or whatever Division happens to have the job, you are the Commander Striking Forces of the Seventh Fleet, and this makes you a vital part of the forces used in the emergency war plans in a big way. You have to be familiar with them and you are constantly having training exercises which you make as meaningful as you can. So we went through several exercises of that sort.

Miss Kitchen: What carrier were you on during this time?

Admiral Lee: I had to move around between several ships, but I was on the KEARSARGE, and the BENNINGTON, and the TICONDEROGA in the process of my CarDivFive career.

I remember one training exercise which might be of some significance. (It was classified at the time. It may still be classified and should be checked before any publication is made.) As ComCarDiv Five, in one of our routine drills, not specifically a part of our emergency plans but as a test of some phases of them, we had to be mindful of the fact that if we were operating in those waters in war we would be under attack from the Russians and the business of concealing the carrier's locations was of considerable importance. Such an exercise in testing concealment, a minor phase of that kind of thing, was ordered and I was on one team and another group took the part of the enemy.

I had come to the conclusion, knowing my Japan pretty well, that there were some places in topography of Japan which could make it difficult for people to know electronically what was happening in the coastal waters. Parts of northern Honshu, the big island of Japan, have high mountains that plunge precipitately into the water and the water is a hundred feet deep just twenty feet off shore. Big ships can cruise right in close. This is highly unusual for an eighty thousand ton ship. There are also some rocky islands around there that partially conceal that area from the sea. I concluded that after launching my attacks, my next measure was to safeguard my force from being apprehended by ostensibly Russian forces coming from the north and west. I elected to take the carrier and our two small destroyers into this spot, and we simply went in and cruised for about forty-eight hours at about five or six knots and about fifty yards off the shore of this large mountain range which blanked off all the electronic communication. While there we went into complete electronic silence. They never got us, right in the harbors of Japan which would be the last place we could ever be expected to be. Nobody ever located us. There were several U. S. Air Force planes involved in the enemy team. They never spotted us visually and their radars were never able to pick us up in such close proximity to the land mass. We also employed some other electronic devices which would indicate that we weren't there.

It worked. However, it never seemed to make much impression on anybody. The critics said it was all a fluke and you couldn't base actual plans on that. I agree, but to me it was an indication that innovation, as history has often shown, sometimes wins. Of course you might lose and so you never know until you try it in war.

Miss Kitchen: Did you get an E for winning?

Admiral Lee: No, we got nothing. It's merely an observation, and interesting sidelight.

Miss Kitchen: It brings up the point that if somebody is involved in a position of extreme responsibiility that their background and experience is going to prove invaluable.

Admiral Lee: It might be. You never can tell what will happen. Innovation and doing the unexpected is still something that will often pay off.

Miss Kitchen: When did you become an admiral?

Admiral Lee: That happened when I assumed command of Carrier Division Fourteen, in '52. In those days they did it differently. I was selected for admiral and given an admiral's job, but I continued on as a captain for about half the time I was Commander Carrier Division Fourteen. I was given the title of Commodore, verbally, but wore a captain's uniform and drew a captain's pay. This is because you had to wait until a vacancy occurred in the rank of admiral. Nowadays, they do what is called "frock" them. They let admiral selectees wear an admiral's uniform and call them admirals, even though they are only getting a captain's pay. We have a lot of them in that status now.

On my way back from the Western Pacific, as Commander Carrier Division Five, I was in the BENNINGTON. We were lucky in being sent down to Australia for the annual celebration of what they call Coral Sea Memorial Week. It's the official commemoration of the Battle of the Coral Sea by the Australian government. They hold it every year because they think that battle was the turning point in the war - it prevented the Japanese from coming into Australia. They make a big fuss about it and they usually have an American representation, one way or another: I was detailed to help in this particular year. Admiral Stump was the Commander-in-Chief Pacific Fleet at the time, and he flew down and gave a speech for one evening and left the next day. I was there for the whole week, which was pretty strenous because the Australians are pretty strenous people.

One incident, possibly historically newsworthy, occurred on the day that we left Australia. This is another example of my troubles and pleasures with the press. During our last two or three days of Coral Sea Week, we were tied up to a dock in Sydney, and the Memorial Hospital of Sydney was holding its annual campaign to raise funds to support the hospital. This is done largely with the cooperation of the University of Sydney which is a great university there and affiliated with the hospital. The students go through all sorts of charades and escapades – mostly designed to raise money and publicity for the hospital fund. In their Australian exuberance they do some pretty extraordinary things. One thing that happened was that they kidnapped the Lord Mayor of Sydney, the head civic official. They kidnapped him bodily, took him off into a small house, and kept him prisoner for three days and nobody knew where he was, and nobody could find him. On the second day after his disappearance, they took his clothes and put them on a dummy and hung it from the middle span of the Sydney Bay Bridge. This is an example of the lengths they go to. Then they said that they would ransom the Lord Mayor for so many Australian pounds for the hospital fund.

As part of the publicity, which I had gone along with, they arranged to have a pirate crew come and capture the BENNINGTON just before we sailed. Then they would extract from the crew a farewell contribution for the hospital fund. This would be done by people all dressed up as pirates, who would come in a little boat just before dawn, come aboard and capture the ship. It was all supposed to be a surprise and you got carried away with the game and the spirit of the times. I was told about it; the skipper was told about it; the Executive Officer knew about it; the Officer of the Deck knew about it: and practically nobody else knew about it. We were prepared to have them come on and capture the Officer of the Deck, and then at reveille the pirates would announce that the ship was captured and at the breakfast mess tables a collection would be taken as ransom for being captured. It was a joke all the way around, with publicity - photographers and so forth. One guy that didn't get the news was the Chief Petty Officer who had the after boat gangway watch, Junior Officer of the Deck. We had a forward gangway which we thought the pirate boat was going to use, but they came to the after gangway. It was dark and they weren't observed and came aboard and captured the Junior Officer of the Deck. This man, a Chief Petty Officer, didn't know about the scheme but he knew something was screwy because they were dressed in medieval costumes, black eye patches, and that sort of thing. So he went tearing across the other side of the deck shouting to the Officer of the Deck. The Officer of the Deck then tried to tell him the story, but unbeknownst to the two of them, and in cahoots with some of the enlisted crew of the BENNINGTON, who were all about the age of the university students with whom they had been pals for a week of Coral Sea celebrations, some of the pirates had been met by a pal in the crew who took them down to the damage control station. There they sounded the general alarm. This was thrity minutes before reveille, and General Quarters sounded all over the ship. The skipper didn't expect that and I didn't expect it. There was a great deal of confusion. Things finally got explained, and that was it. The photographers arrived and took pictures, and we gave them the ransom money.

There was a Time Magazine stringer in Sydney. He wasn't there at the scene; he was up in his bunk somewhere miles away, but he heard about this. He talked to some students, and he wrote a story and put in on the cable to Time Magazine which came out with a vivid description of this incident, allegedly portraying that the security of the American Navy had proved completely inadequate: a bunch of student pirates had been able to capture the ship and get down into the damage control station and sound the general alarm without anybody knowing about it. Of course, all of this was basically true to a degree. But they blew it up as much as they could to make a good story.

We sailed right after this happened. We didn't know what had happened in the press, and certainly didn't know what was going to come out in Time Magazine. We were on our way back to Hawaii when the first thing I realized I got a hot message from Admiral Stump, who said, "Explain in detail the circumstances in which your ship was risked, and so forth, as reported in the press." I thought at first that Admiral Stump was being facetious. He and I were good friends, had known each other for years, and I thought he was just pulling my leg a little bit. So I said, "Gee, it wasn't in the press we got. What did the press say? Give us a little dope." It was a person to person message between him and me. It wasn't on the message traffic. He came back with a second message which indicated that he wasn't joking at all, that this was a serious thing; Time Magazine had said these things, and he quoted from the Time article.

I tried to straighten it out and tell him as much as I could over the wires, and I said, "I'll tell you the whole thing when I get back, and I don't think you'll be mad, but for goodness sake it wasn't in any sense a real loss of security, and Time Magazine was wrong to blow it up this way. Do the best you can with the press from that point of view, and I'll give you all the details when I get to Honolulu a week from now."

That didn't make Admiral Stump very happy. He was mad at me then and I think he may still be mad at me for that particular incident. He thought it was a violation of security because this incident might have been done by real Communists.

Miss Kitchen: It could have been, and they could have taken people down and wrecked the ship I suppose.

Admiral Lee: Possibly, but this could happen tomorrow right here in San Diego.

It was very colorful, but I was very unhappy at the time. That practically ends my CarDiv Five career. The rest of it was routine.

My next duty was as the Chief of Naval Air Technical Training with headquarters in Memphis, Tennessee. It was a job which was something of a mystery to me before I got there, having never heard much about it and having had little to do with its workings in my previous naval career.

The Naval Air Technical Training Command is under an admiral - there are three other training commands under the Chief of Naval Training with headquarters in Pensacola. The job of the Naval Air Technical Training Command is to receive each year from the high schools - sometimes high school dropouts and from grade schools - all over the United States about fifty or sixty thousand young men who join the Navy (in those years) as recruits and come to Memphis directly after eight weeks of boot training. Memphis' job is to take these men, give them tests to find out what their capabilities are, and then to steer them into and train them in a professional job in the aviation Navy where they can best use their talents and capabilities.

Miss Kitchen: They've had tests at boot camp before they came?

Admiral Lee: Yes, they've had some, but they've had no assignment. We had the results of the boot camp tests. The boot camps didn't determine what they should do in aviation, because they knew we would further screen them for their aviation capabilities. They gave the full range of basic tests and we had all that plus others related to aviation that we did ourselves.

We ran a large complex of schools in Memphis. The Training Command was put there because it was the center of the United States, mid-way between each coast. We thought it would save railroad fare that way, and it may have done that but it had other handicaps. Administratively, in retrospect, and if we could start all over again we could make a good case for putting it in two parts - one on the East Coast and one on the West Coast. But it's there in Memphis and the investment is huge. It works very well, and has many assets.

We had an average population of about fourteen thousand young mem (and women) at Memphis, and in the other schools under my direct command as Chief of Naval Air Technical Training, which were not located in Memphis itself. I had the control of all of them. For instance - the boiler tender schools were in Philadelphia, and the aircraft control tower operations people, the FAA types, were in Olathe, Kansas. Others were in San Diego, and so on.

This brought me in a number of ways face to face with the educational facts of life in the United States. We were processing more than fifty thousand a year in aviation alone. We were sharing this experience with the fifty thousand or more that weren't in aviation ratings, but went directly under the Chief of Naval Personnel with whom we worked hand in glove in training procedures. We had a complete interchange of information. We had this also with the corresponding schools of the Air Force and the Army, which were bigger than ours and and in the same business. In all, we were looking at some two hundred and fifty to three hundred thousand young men a year, who were being taken out of the high schools of the United States, and given to us to make soldiers and sailors and airmen out of them.

The product of the American school system, as we saw it, wasn't a good one. In the first place, we found that the average high school graduates were undereducated. By that I mean that they had spent eight, ten, twelve years in school during the most efficient, spongelike part of their lives for the absorption of instruction and information; they hadn't been offered nearly as much as they could have absorbed. We were way behind other nations in this in several respects.

The second thing we found was that they were much like the American prisoners of war in Korea. The North Koreans found that their American prisoners had vague ideas about citizenship, patriotism, the U. S. government, the responsibilities of citizens, things of that sort. We had the Korean findings confirmed right there in Memphis in our incoming students.

The third thing we found out was that the quality of the school systems of the United States ranged from very good to very bad. We found that the little red school house wasn't worth a damn as an educational institution, although it may have had some good aspects otherwise. We found out that one school district and another contiguous school district in the same state were often far different. In big cities we could tell you which were the one or two best high schools. We found that many cities designate certain high schools for gifted children, and if we could get the graduates of that high school, we had it made. We found that a graduate of a high school in the state of New York, who got his diploma, was a very valuable man or woman to us. We knew we could use him. This included all of Harlem. The catch was that a graduation certificate from a high school in New York was given only to those who had passed all of the required courses and the required courses included the fundamentals. If they didn't pass they didn't get a diploma; they got a certificate of completion saying that they had finished four years. We found that several states on the average were much better than others. We found that there were considerable differences in the schools of various states. As I recall New Hampshire, New York, Iowa, Idaho were much better than other states. It wasn't always the wealthy state who had the best schools, although it was a factor that the wealthy states in general were better than the less wealthy states.

After some personal research I concluded that many of the deficiencies had to do with the educational system of the United States as a whole; that the hierarchy of the teaching establishment had the principal responsibility; that what they were doing and how they were doing it didn't seem to be nearly as good as it could have been for America.

I was seeing this in my own children in Memphis. I had been a member of the PTA and had soon found out that there is an agreement, a conspiracy almost, between the NEA, the National Education Association, office of Federal Education (which is now the "E" of HEW) and the PTA, as to how our schools and how education are going to be run in the United States. In 1955, the PTA, by its charter, was not and from its inception had never been allowed to look into what should be taught or was being taught, or how it should be taught in the schools. All it could do is to see that the teachers lounge was well appointed, that the swings in the playground didn't squeak, that the piano was tuned, and that kind of thing. But they couldn't get into what's taught and how it's taught, and I believe that is still the case today.

Another insight into our school systems was afforded me while at Memphis. Shortly before I became Chief of Naval Air Technical Training, Mr. Eisenhower, as a result of Sputnik, had started the first federally financed program of public education in order to strengthen the teaching of science and mathematics in the high schools. This was done in part as a result of the findings in the Armed Forces recruit training stations that great numbers of young men had little or no knowledge of science or mathematics. We had to give too many of them high school courses in these subjects before we could start to use them as soldiers and sailors.

A part of this program, by some strange aberration of our bureaucratic systems, gave to the Air Force the task of taking high school mathematics and science teachers around to various military installations and showing them how great was the need for increased science and mathematics in the schools. This chore the Air Force had delegated to the Civil Air Patrol. We happened to be a big center for recruit training in the central part of the United States, so the Civil Air Patrol brought these teachers to Memphis and let them spend three days with us as a part of their tour. During ever spring and every fall vacation in the schools we got a succession of two or three visits of about a hundred and fifty high school science and mathematics teachers from all over the middle west. They looked at our schools, at our methods of instruction, grading systems, et cetera. And they were surprised and impressed that we were teaching so much in such a short period of time without benefit of professional teachers. As a matter of fact, we were doing it for the most part with petty officers, and chief petty officers. They were envious of the discipline in our class rooms which they said was impossible for them to achieve. I used to argue with them about this, saying it could be achieved if the will was there.

Another thing of great interest to them was that our "teachers" were given only a short course of about four weeks in pedagogy before being assigned to teaching duty and then subjected to a coaching process which could go on for as long as a year. This scheme consisted in introducing phony students into their classes, who were really competent instructors. After sitting in the new teachers class for a few sessions the instructor would reveal himself and tell the teacher what he was doing wrong, where he was weakest, and where he should strengthen his teaching. The new teacher did know that such a spy system existed, but he didn't know when it was going to happen to him. All of our enlisted teachers were highly in favor of this system - said it was invaluable. This spy system the visiting math and science teacher found valuable, but said that it was absolutely forbidden in the American educational system.

Miss Kitchen: Is this system which you initiated?

Admiral Lee: No, it was there when I came. I think it was widely used in our military schools. We all interchanged information all the time.

But this exposure to undereducated kids, being able to do so much with them in such a short period of time, finding that they were weak in self discipline and that they longed for discipline, and finding that they were weak in their appreciation of citizen responsibilities - all this made a tremendous impression on me and, I think, on anybody else that got involved in the program. Professional teachers would come and look at us and say, "We wish we could do it like you can." I thought it incredible that they felt they couldn't.

I mention all this product of my two years in Memphis because it got so many of us interested in our leadership programs and our morale programs, about what we could do to improve them. At this time we started a leadership and citizenship training program nation wide. People were upset everywhere about the attitudes of the prisoners of war in Korea. As a consequence of this, and because many citizens had learned about our basic school systems in the Aviation Navy, people came to us and said, "What can we do to strengthen our community schools and get a better education for our kids? You seem to be doing better."

As a result of this, Admiral Goldthwaite, who was then the Chief of Naval Air Training, took the ball, and the naval air stations of the Aviation Training Command became leaders of a program to tell more people about what we were doing with the Navy recruits. We held seminars on naval installations (and subsequently on military installations of all the services inviting citizens groups to come and look at what we were doing and to discuss the problems. We showed what we were teaching in our leadership programs about the roots of Communism, the reasons for why we had to be strong, what we might do to make better citizens, better sailors, soldiers, and so forth. Because a few of the lecturers and the guests had sort of John Birch reputations, some liberal citizens found them questionable. This led to the Fulbright Memorandum, which said that the armed forces of the United States were involved in politics and in political indoctrination of Americans about foreign policy and domestic policy and that this must be stopped immediately. Fulbright said that the officers of the armed services were not qualified by knowledge or education to talk about these things, much less try to indoctrinate other American citizens about them. This caused a big stir in lots of places. The Fulbright memorandum is far from dead, nor is Fulbright. I believe he still has the same views and his anti-military attitudes make difficulties for the armed forces.

I believe it all goes back to our failure of our educational system in the United States to do what it might have done, could have done, and didn't do, and which it isn't doing yet. We are seeing the proof of it in the colleges and high schools of 1970.

All of what I've said thus far about my observations of the American educational system made a profound influence on me and I have done what I could in subsequent years to bring about improvements in the educational system. I've convinced it is not as good as it could be and should be. I've found in every community where I've lived that it is almost the same. I still find high school graduates who are undereducated, who have a wide smattering of courses which, collectively, produce little real education. You find kids getting out of college and out of high schools with practically no motivation or sense of civic responsibility. I know that's there a large number of people to whom this doesn't apply, but the problem is that there are far too many to whom it does.

Miss Kitchen: When I was in the recruit training command for women, my observation was that young girls that age, eighteen, really loved the discipline. They liked to know what they were supposed to do, and they liked the feeling of having accomplished whatever it was they knew they had to do.

Admiral Lee: This was the same thing that we constantly encountered in the Training Command. Later I had three years as the Chief of Naval Air Training and I continued to find that these same observations were valid. In addition, as CNATRA, I had the additional job of recruiting in the colleges to find officer candidates for aviation duty. At that time these constituted more than half of the officers taken in each year in the Navy. We had a number of recruiting teams under my command on college campuses. I had long talks with them about their recruiting efforts.

After two years as Chief of Naval Air Technical Training I had about eighteen months or two years with Admiral Dennison in the Atlantic Fleet, and then became Chief of Naval Air Training, who bosses the Chief of Naval Air Technical Training.

Miss Kitchen: They seem to fit together.

Admiral Lee: They do. It was a good continuation.

As the Chief of Naval Air Training I also bossed the Chief of Naval Air Reserve Training - the weekend warrior program at the Naval Air Reserve Stations all over the United States.

I had had the flight training program too, which is divided into basic training and advanced training. This comprised quite a large empire, if you want to call it that, with many installations nationwide. I traveled a great deal.

As I mentioned one of our big jobs was recruiting aviation officers. We had to use every trick of the trade. I visited campuses and saw what it took and was impressed again by the shallowness of much of college education.

If I can expand just a bit more. We were taking in officers with only as much as two years college training, because those were all we could get. The great pressure, of course, was to get college graduates because the sheepskin psychosis heavily pervaded all phases of society in the United States. We found, somewhat to our surprise however, that our best officers came from among the two year college people, not out of the four year college graduates. We also found that by far our best officers came from other than the Ivy League colleges. I think there were several reasons for this. One was that many of the people who finished two years were crackerjack people. Many of them knew they wanted to fly, and of course, that was nice for us. The only thing they lacked was money to finish their last two years of school. But they had motivation and they had many other fine qualities. A fellow like that was worth ten times as much to us as the fellow who had finished four years of college, had been subsidized by his parents through the whole thing, and who had not taken any particularly solid major but had drifted through various types of this and that - medieval history, landscape gardening, music appreciation, and so forth. After four years of it, he still didn't know what he wanted to be or why, but he had heard about the aviation program. He'd signed up for it, thinking he might as well try that as anything else - it was a paying job. As between the two of them, I believe the two year people made our best officers by far.

The pressure of the sheepskin psychosis, this adulation of a college degree was so strong that we were forced (not by the Aviation Navy's wish, I don't believe, because we did not advocate it) to take only college graduates as young officers. In so doing we miss an awful lot of fine young people. I continually advocated, as Chief of Naval Air Training, taking these young men, spending the time to teach them to fly, letting them serve two or three years, and then looking them over again. By that time they will be a little more mature. You can pick the good ones and give them two or more years of college at the Navy's expense, and you'll have a better team as a whole. Other factors prevented this.

As Chief of Naval Air Training, I was greated interested in the Reserve Training Command. Here again I had a lot of contacts with civilians - the weekend warriors. I traveled a good deal to reserve training stations, and was able to talk to all kinds of people in the reserves. They are basically solid citizens in their own community, mindful of their civilian problems, and mindful also of the many limitations which we had in trying to keep a reserve program going in a society becoming increasingly indifferent to the needs of national security. Some of the officers in our reserves were in it for "what's in it for me" rather than because of the patriotic angle. This always distressed me a little bit. We subsidized them with money and that's what they wanted mostly. It was worth it, but we could hope for better motives.

While at Memphis, and as I grew more and more aware of the great dividends of good leadership, I started an informal Newsletter to all of the Commanding Officers under my command. It was devoted mostly to morale building and leadership training. I recommended that all or parts of it be passed down the chain of command to the executive officers, head of departments, and division officers - they being the key links in the leadership chain.

I continued this practice in my next job as Chief of Staff to Admiral Dennison, Commander-in-Chief of the Atlantic Fleet. There we had what we called the LANTLEADER; it was signed by Dennison, but I did almost all the writing and editing.

Later, as Chief of Naval Air Training - CNATRA - I continued the practice. In the Training Command it was called CNATRA Dope. It was sent to every commanding officer, several hundred of them. They included the commanding officers of all of the Naval Air Reserve Training Squadrons. I used this vehicle to impress on the commanding officer his own key importance to everything that went on in his own command and in the Navy, because he was the man responsible absolutely for the performance of the unit. I stressed that he must know his subordinate officers well and keep them informed, giving them copies of CNATRA Dope when he wanted to, and even getting it down to the division officers and the leading chiefs, so that they would have a sense of cohesion and know what was going on in the Navy, how the top people were thinking. Oddly it seemed to me that there was no other publication like that in the Navy in which this sort of thing was done. Dope was very successful. Admiral Dennison also seemed to like LANTLEADER very much when I was writing it for him. In Admiral Dennison's case, where we had a very large command, he limited distribution to the flag officers under his command but he encouraged them to reprint it or use any parts of it for wider dissemination.

In these newsletters we were free to talk about anything informally, free from the gobbledegook of Pentagonese: to give the unadulterated word; to interpret things and explain things which were about to come through officially from me and might be understood better with an informal rationale made known beforehand.

I also included with the newsletter two supplements. One of these was the public speeches made by naval, military, or national leaders which seemed to me to be pertinent to some of the problems besetting the Navy and national policy. The other form of supplement was a press clipping service selected from the point of view of naval and national security interests

Miss Kitchen: I think that's wonderful. I never was part of any command where I saw that done.

Admiral Lee: I tried to sell it in other places, and it has been done in other places. It usually falls down I have found for lack of personal interest by the man at the top. If you don't have that, if it's just delegated to some subordinate officer, who can't write with authority and can't say things because he is afraid his boss is going to object or won't think it's right, or doesn't make him look right, or something of that sort - then it gradually deteriorates to something that's not very readable. My letters were written in the first person singular for me or Dennison.

I also used to keep a card file (and still do) of famous quotations on notable thoughts or quotable quotes. I would fill up empty spaces in the newsletter with these. This personal newsletter was, I believe, very successful. It made the commanding officers in all areas of the command all over the U. S. feel that they were a part of the team. I am sure that it well paid my efforts in trying to get things done that I wanted to get done; at least many people told me so. I've seen similar things like this done in big industry and in other organizations.

I found that writing and editing these letters, although it took a considerable part of my time, was also valuable educational process for me. I felt I was doing myself good, and doing the service good, by making myself a better person, by deciding which were the important things that should be disseminated, by throwing out the rest, and getting the news out to my command rather than perhaps just getting people mixed up by a lack of news. You can't just toss things off in a hurry - and I'm not thinking of the beauty of the grammar - you must make sure that you are saying things that are factually correct, things that are not going to steer people into avenues of thinking which are really just your own and may or may not be right. In other words, trying to keep it as accurate and objective as I could.

The Chief of Naval Air Training's job is a big one. It's highly centralized and differs from training in the rest of the Navy. Actually it was Admiral Radford who organized the Naval Air Training Command, and not without considerable blood, sweat, and tears in the process. In the non-aviation Navy, the training is conducted almost wholly under BuPers. In BuPers this particular responsibility is not as well channelized, and responsibility is diffused in the large bureaucratic mass of paper work in BuPers. However all the basic problems remain the same. Naval Aviation doesn't do anything essentially different and is always consulting back and forth with the non-aviation Navy in training matters. There is no basic sense of rivalry or dispute about methods. We were both free to do what we wanted to do, and I think it wasn't at all a bad organization from that point of view.

Several times, through the years, the recommendation has been made that the system of the Naval Air Training Command be extended to the rest of the Navy and taken out of Washington.

One of the beauties of the Air Training Command was that its headquarters was a thousand miles away and, for that reason, better in many ways. There were some handicaps, but they were more than outweighed by the advantages. This business of establishing a training command in the field for the entire Navy, so to speak, always somehow got bogged down. There were arguments on both sides, and so it never seemed to come to fruition for that reason.

(Since the above was said - the change was actually made in 1971. F.L.)

Miss Kitchen: It seems to me that because of the somehow integrated aviation type training you would have had better control than the bureaus.

Admiral Lee: We had a more unified control. For instance, in the Bureau of Naval Personnel the procurement of the college graduates for the line officers, other than aviation, in the Navy was parcelled in many little cubby holes in the Bureau, and some of them didn't know what the others were doing. They weren't always well geared with the other parts of training, enlisted training, and so forth. The reserve training was completely independent and entirely different. We, in aviation, had a simple direct wiring diagram which proved to be effective and I think it still is.

Miss Kitchen: It was such a big job I wonder if you might expand more on it. I know that it involved thousands of people and it was nation wide.

Admiral Lee: It was a big job. It was interesting and I enjoyed it. We had an aircraft carrier, the LEXINGTON, as a training carrier based in Pensacola. We had most of our aviation training fields for the training command in the southeastern part of the United States, principally in four big areas - Jacksonville, Pensacola, Meridian, Mississippi and Corpus Christi, Texas. There were many small activities all over the country in addition to those.

We trained not only naval aviators, but we had other training jobs that supplied the whole Navy and weren't peculiar just to aviation. For instance, we trained all the photographers for the Navy in naval air photographic schools.

We trained all of the flight surgeons of the Navy, both those who became naval aviators, and those who received flight training, and those who had a six months course for all doctors who were absorbed in the Navy by the draft for the most part, and said they would be willing to become flight surgeons although I think most of them didn't have a good idea what it was all about. The school for flight surgeons was at Pensacola, and under the command of a dynamic flight surgeon, Captain Phoebus. To me the embryo flight surgeons were an interesting microcosm of the medical profession. I saw a lot of them.

They were all doctors just out of internships and very eager-beaverish. We gave them a course of indoctrination in military life. This wasn't done for the other doctors that came into the Navy; they just drafted directly out of medical school and were sent to a hospital or a ship as a doctor and that was it.

I continually through the years heard expressions of gratitude from the flight surgeons for the fact that we took time to give them military indoctrination. They didn't know what to do with a sword, how to buckle it on, or when or who to salute, insignia, rank, et cetera.

We made them all pass the same test for physical fitness as naval aviators. It seems an astonishing statistic, but about eighty percent of the people we got as candidates for flight surgeon training could not swim. We insisted that they all be good swimmers and pass the swimming test. Some of them had a pretty grim time learning enough to get by the test. They spent many hours in the tank, but they all said they were grateful for it.

We were active in the program for training in citizenship, which I mentioned that Admiral Goldthwaite had started, and which incurred the wrath of Senator Fulbright and others. Even though we were enjoined not to do anything in this field, we were petitioned in many cases by community leaders, with whom we had formerly worked in close cooperation to participate with them in one way or another. It was embarrassing and maddening to have to tell a naval officer that he couldn't go out and talk to the Kiwanis Club on this particular subject because it was controversial and the Pentagon forbade it. We were going on with our own in-house courses of indoctrination in basic communism.

I might mention that the Naval Air Training Command was active in earlier years in helping to establish a compulsory requirement of one semester on "Communism vs Americanism" in high school for all Florida public school students. I believe it is still a part of the standard requirement in the Florida high schools. The Florida law has also become a model for several other states.

Miss Kitchen: I've just read the citation that accompanied Admiral Lee's Distinguished Service Medal, and he makes the comment that these were routine duties. Would you expand more on that?

Admiral Lee: People often get Distinguished Service Medals and the like because a good program was developed by some subordinate in the command and which turns out well and the boss gets the credit. Sometimes they result, for the most part, from improvement to on-going programs, which of course is the duty of every officer to do. If an officer is considered by some board of awards at the end of his tour, especially when you get fairly senior, it's more or less an endorsement of the command as a whole rather than of a particular individual, I believe - not always, but in many cases.

Miss Kitchen: When did you become Vice Admiral?

Admiral Lee: When I was ordered to the staff of Admiral Dennison as Commander-in-Chief of the Atlantic Fleet and the Atlantic Command, about 1962.

Miss Kitchen: Do you think you have finished your comments relating to your duty in Pensacola?

Admiral Lee: I would like to go back and mention one thing. Leadership has always been one of my great fetishes, so to speak. When I was Chief of Naval Air Technical Training I was working with Admiral Goldthwaite. He, with my help, established a CPO leadership school in Pensacola under me as Chief of Naval Air Technical Training, where it still remains, although I would say the leadership is not a subject for technical training. This resulted from my visit and several visits by others to some of the U. S. Air Force Strategic Air Commands schools for non-commissioned officer leadership training - particularly the one at Barksdale Field, Louisiana, which had been established by a dynamic Air Force officer. This school was highly successful and has been through the years. It's been imitated in other parts of the Navy, Army, and Air Force. The original motive was to take the fairly senior petty officer who probably made petty officer too rapidly for his own good in World War II and to give him some indoctrination in the Navy as a whole. We called it, bringing them up to date in the techniques of leadership and responsibility, the role of the

Navy, and so forth. Our school at Pensacola was visited by literally hundreds of SecNav guests and visitors who came through Pensacola and wanted to take a look at it.

We treated these petty officers just like they were boot seamen. We wouldn't let their families come with them to Pensacola. The school was open to all the training commands, and students were drawn from all over the United States, nominated by their commanding officers. If the student came from a Pensacola command and his family was right there in Pensacola, he was put in the Leadership School barracks and couldn't see his wife or family for the two or three weeks he was there. We just treated them like rookies to begin with, and gradually eased up. They all said that they hated it in the first week, and they thought it was the best thing that ever happened to them in the thrid week. This is the way it's still going.

These middle aged petty officers were shown that theirs was a unique responsibility in the chain of command, that they had a great job to do, that the stakes in world history were important, and that nothing less than the highest standards would obtain. We made these people make up their bunks, shine the floor under their bunks, shine their shoes, keep their uniforms immaculate - far beyond anything they had ever known befor

For the most part our standards were much higher than anywhere else in the Navy. The students were something like the plebes at West Point and Annapolis only more so; they had to be top perfect. It worked and it's still working and it's something which could well be expanded today.

Going back to my duty before I was Chief of Naval Air Training, I had almost two years under Admiral Dennison, who was Commander-in-Chief Atlantic Fleet, and Commander-in-Chief of the United States Atlantic Command, composed of the U. S. Army, Navy and Air Forces in the Atlantic area. At the same time Admiral Dennison wore a hat as Supreme Allied Commander Atlantic in the NATO organization. I had nothing to do with the NATO part of his command. I was Dennison's Deputy for CinCLant, the Atlantic Command of the United States forces, and his Chief of Staff for the United States Atlantic Fleet.

I had known Admiral Dennison for years, and I had always had great admiration for him and still do. He gave me a free hand and only stopped me when I was going off on some tangent which needed being stopped. He traveled a great deal and with his many high responsibilites in Europe for NATO in which I was not concerned. For this reason I perhaps had a larger degree of independent responsibility than I would have had otherwise.

My time with CinCLant was during troublous years in history. We had several command organizational problems, which Washington was trying to unscramble. There was much fuss about the creation of the Strike Command, which became one of the unified commands of the armed forces of the United States and to which the Navy, at its inception, was considerably opposed. Other people were opposed also, but it had many devoted supporters. There was much staff discussion, argument, study, and so forth on whether or not the command was desirable and how it affected the Atlantic Command, which it did very considerably. It took away the geographical responsibility for all of Africa, which CinCLant had had, and gave it to the Strike Command, which didn't seem to make sense in many ways. (The Strike Command was dis-establihsed in the summer of 1971.)

We also had jurisdictional disputes with the Air Force and with our own Pacific Command on the organization for the defenses of Panama. These brought about changes which ended up in the creation of what came to be called CinCSouth, with headquarters in Panama. It had the responsibility for all of the military aid programs in Latin America, which theretofore had been separately under the Navy, Air Force, and Army departments in Washington. CinCSouth also was created more or less against the recommendation of the Navy. It has had its troubles since. (It was dis-established in 1971.)

These were the years of troubles in Panama, caused by efforts of the Panamanians to have more money from and more ownership of the Canal Zone. Fighting occurred in our Embassy, on the school campuses of Canal Zone schools, and so forth. They were trying times for us in the military, because we felt that too many concessions were being made to Panama that were deleterious to our own national security. I think the years have proven we still haven't solved the problem there by making these concessions. If anything things are worse, and today in 1970 we are suffering from some of the decisions that were made at that time, which we opposed strongly, but which were overruled by higher authority. Today we find ourselves with the possibilities of a new canal, new treaties, which have grave implications for history. We have divided camps in our own government, mostly the State Department against the rest of the government, as to what is the best thing to do. I've been following these developments in detail as much as I could through the years, and I can't say that the outlook is a happy one.

Two significant operations occurred while I was with CinCLant. The first was the Congo revolution when Belgium walked out of the Belgian Congo on twenty-four hours notice, and the latter was declared a republic and all sorts of unhappy things happened.

We had establihsed Joint Task Force Four in preparation for such an event, because it looked like we were going to have trouble. Joint Task Force Four was a headquarters organization to be moved to the area in case a crisis came. It was assembled at Fort Monroe, across from Norfolk, under Admiral Dennison as CinCLant. This was then in the Atlantic Command's area of responsibility and before the establishment of the Strike Command.

When things actually got hot in the Congo, Joint Task Force Four went into operation and did much good work. The people on this staff had studied every aspect of what the United States government would have to do, the air lift phases of it, and so forth. The Atlantic Fleet controlled the assembling of UN troops in the Congo from other places, notably India, Pakistan, and

Thailand, and brought them to the Congo on Navy ships. An unforseen difficulty arose when they put many more troops on board these ships than we thought wise to take. Many of them were Mohammedans and they wouldn't eat anything but Mohammedan diets and had other customs which were strange to normal Navy transport life. They all got there successfully and were taken home successfully, courtesy of U. S. Navy, without any supplemental appropriations for doing it.

Miss Kitchen: Did you go over to the Congo?

Admiral Lee: At that time, no. I have since been there.

We learned many lessons in the Congo affair. Although the Congo extends to the Atlantic at the mouth of the Congo River, there is really no way of supplying it by sea. There's nothing decent in the way of a port at the mouth of the river. There is a long stretch of rapids at Kinshasa (ex-Leopoldville), so you can't use the upper reaches of one of the largest rivers in the world for any meaningful water transport. There are several places up river where you have to make a portage around rapids and falls.

A second major handicap was the paucity of air transport facilities and the lack of freedom to fly over other countries into the Congo. This became a key point. At one time when the United Nations troops in the Congo were in pretty dire straits and military supplies were badly needed, there was only one air route we could use to send material into the Congo.

This involved using Wheelus Field in Libya, and the field at Omdurman in the Sudan. The air distances are long and practically all of the black African ex-colonial nations were against the UN operations. We couldn't get permission to fly anywhere except over Libya and the Sudan. If we hadn't had a lease on Wheelus in Libya (which we no longer hold) and if the Sheik who had just taken power by a coup in Sudan hadn't gone against the wishes of most of his advisors, we wouldn't have been able to use these two vital fueling stops. Without them there would have been no significant air supply into the Congo, and an awful lot depended on it.

This sealift of troops and airlift of cargo give a little sidelight on the importance of bases, air rights, ports, navigable water, freedom to use the seas, et cetera, in a crisis situation. I believe we will be more and more aware of this as time goes on.

Miss Kitchen: Didn't the Bay of Pigs happen during the time that you were at CinCLant?

Admiral Lee: Yes. This was one of the two things that I mentioned. The Bay of Pigs did occur. I suppose many reams will be written about the Bay of Pigs as the years go by.

Miss Kitchen: Did it affect you in your operation?

Admiral Lee: Very much. Cuba is in the American Atlantic Command - in CinCLant's area of responsibility. Any U. S. military operations undertaken there were the responsibility of Admiral Dennison. We, of course, were very close to our naval and military attaches throughout Latin America. We were always dealing with them. We were aware of the problems in Cuba. We had distressing reports coming to us in various ways - some of them second and third hand, but some of them pretty direct, which indicated that there was a lot going on in Cuba, and that our way of dealing with these current problems wasn't right. We knew that our ambassador in Havana was at odds with the State Department. We knew that many responsible people were unhappy with the way that our embassy was acting under orders from the State Department. At one stage the Naval Attache in Havana flew up and asked to see Admiral Dennison. I was there when he saw him. He broke down in tears in Admiral Dennison's office describing the problem he was having at the embassy because he and the ambassador couldn't get things done which they thought needed to be done, which were opposed by the State Department who were supporting Castro. We had all kinds of small indications of this which made us unhapp;

We had on our CinCLant staff a representative of the CIA, who was an officer in uniform. He was a reserve officer working for CIA on active duty, and assigned to Dennison as a CIA liaison officer. This officer knew about the decision of the CIA to support the Bay of Pigs operation, but he was not permitt to tell us about it. At a fairly late stage in the preparations we got word of the Bay of Pigs planning, but not from him or from Washington, but from subordinates in our own fleet command. They were told to turn over supplies to people and in places which they couldn't figure out. It looked suspicious and they queried us as to whether they should do it. This was our first indication of the existance of a U. S. supported operation to liberate Cuba. After questioning Washington about it, Admiral Dennison and myself and an intelligence officer on our staff were told about the Bay of Pigs.

Miss Kitchen: How were you told?

Admiral Lee: By an officer coming down to brief us – one of the top people in CIA. We were amazed. Admiral Burke and the other members of the Joint Chiefs of Staff learned about it only a short time before we did. This had all been done by CIA and we were pretty aghast. It was very far along – we were aghast that we hadn't been cut in earlier; we didn't like the general framework of the plan; we had serious doubts as to how it could succeed; we weren't in agreement with quite a number of phases of it; but we were told that we had no responsibility whatsoever except to support it as ordered. This included immediately getting some additional liaison officers who were to tell us exactly what we would have to do in certain things in support of this operation.

Miss Kitchen: Were you told the complete plan when you were told?

Admiral Lee: No, not the complete plan, but enough about the major framework to let us know in general what the scope was and what all its implications were. We were sort of in a hand wringing stage of saying, "If you're going to do this, let's do it better." But our voices were not heard and I'm sure ours were not the only ones at that time.

Anyway the Atlantic Fleet did participate to a considerable degree in turning over equipment to the free Cubans, helping them in training in minor ways, getting some ships and things outfitted with supplies, supplying other things of that sort.

We knew about it - the Bay of Pigs. We positioned ships of the Atlantic Fleet in the immediate vicinity or in close enough in case of need. One ASW aircraft carrier was very near the scene. We had taken off some of the ASW type of airplane and put a few attack aircraft on the ship for that purpose. The admiral in command of that force, John E. Clark, was cut in on the plan, and told why he was there, but few of the rest of the crew knew about it until just before the landing. Other forces were standing by to help if needed, and we thought they would be needed.

It turned out at the last moment that some significant parts of the plan as we knew it had been cancelled or changed by the White House. The principal one being a change in the location of the landings.

As I recall we were told that any American help which could in any way be identified as American could not be used no matter what the emergency.

During the landings, Admiral Dennison, Admiral Rivero, who was the assistant Chief of Staff, myself, and another five or ten key officers of the staff were in our combat operations center for practically the whole two days - about forty-eight hours. We soon found that we were basically a communications relay station and little else. We weren't asked to make any decisions or give opinions. We sort of deplored what was happening. We were in voice contact at times - mostly, however, the radio message contact was better - with Admiral Clark.

We could hear or read about everything that was said between the Pentagon and Admiral Clark and ourselves. There were often long hiatuses as when we would say something to Admiral Burke and Admiral Burke would say, "Hold," and he would talk to the White House, and the White House would come back, and Burke would say to us, "This is the way it's to be." Or he would initiate the conversation and say, "We are told that this will be done this way and you must do these things." We never heard any of the voices from the White House, but we were told what was told to them and what the reply was.

We were pretty unhappy. It was obvious that if we weren't going to help - and maybe even if we did - there was going to be a tragedy. Some things were done which indicated to us that an operation like that can't be run by remote control, and especially by a person who's not familiar with that type of opertion.

2 Lee - 296

Here's an example. At the last moment, there was a bunch of Cubans - the invading Cubans, the good guys - who managed to get into a boat and escape sure death ashore. They got to a small island on the other shore of the Bay of Pigs, and were signalling for help saying that if nobody came to get them they would soon be lost. There were about thirty or forty of them, I think. They had a good radio and we were hearing that and it looked like something could be done, because it was some distance from the landing beaches.

Washington authorized the carrier to send a boat in and investigate and help if they could. Before that boat could leave, and they didn't know this until they were just about to shove off, they had to stop the preparations in order to remove every scrap of evidence that this was an American boat.

The crew had to be dressed in civilian clothes with nothing that could identify them American, the boat plates had to be taken off, and the names - every scrap of evidence that could be used in a court of law as proof that it was an American boat had to be removed before they could go in to see if there was anything could be done. That took an hour or so to do. They got there and it was too late. They couldn't even find the people.

Miss Kitchen: Is that in the history?

Admiral Lee: I've not read all the histories. It was certainl well known to us. There were other indications. We had fighte planes patrolling, looking at the scene from the air, and the word would come, relayed from Washington, "Ask the pilot of the plane to indicate where the front lines are?" This would go to the Pentagon, sometimes direct to the ship, sometimes to Norfolk and then on the ship, and then from the ship to the pilot. The pilot was probably some little j.g. who had rarely been out of Alabama in his life. He probably was looking at his first combat, and there weren't any discernible front lines. There would be nothing he could say in a meaningful way that would interpret where front lines were to anybody in the White House. This was one of a number of examples of clogging up communications channels in ways that seemed to handicap getting a good job done.

After I left Chief of Naval Air Training, I served as the Commandant of the National War College. Some of the participants in one phase or another in the Bay of Pigs operation were students, or on the staff, or lecturers at the College. The Bay of Pigs were re-hashed in various coffee sessions and informal seminars. The affair was discussed in great length, usually in the context of whether it was the correct way to handle a cold war or Communist aggression.

Often a key point was the role of the President in military command in trying to control tactical things from the White House. Should he talk to a man commanding a tank, or a ship, or an airplane above a battle line? This was a major issue, too, in the Tonkin Gulf business, and the MADDOX.

While we were having these discussions, technical improvements were being installed worldwide at very great expense to perfect our ability to sit in Washington and be able to talk to people all over the world in a crisis. Not only this, but also to know instantly with computer help a mind-numbing mass of knowledge - such that to eighty-two miles southwest of point "x" there was a squad of two officers with six grenades and two recoiless rifles who might be called upon, things like that - fantastic concepts. They were apparently considered as absolutely necessary in order that tachtical decisions could be made by Command centers - could be made by one individual who might be ten or as many as ten thousand miles away.

A tiny incident can lead quickly to touching off an atomic exchange these days, so it is argued that the President must be in a position to make this momentous decision quickly. He can only do it with a great deal of knowledge of what actually is happening. Therefore billions of dollars must go into a communication and computer system which will be able to give him all this knowledge.

I, and others, argue that the trouble is that no President no military officer in Washington can begin to absorb the last two or three weeks of happenings in that particular area and relate them to the actual incident, and thus to make a meaningful judgement. He's just as likely to make a bad decision, touched off by misinterpretation of a tiny thing as obvious as day or night to the man on the spot. As a matter of fact, the President might not even realize that it was night at the scene, and make the assumption that the eye witnesses were able to see two hundred yards when they couldn't because it was dark.

These are just quick samples of a major problem that continues today, and probably will for the indefinite future.

In the last two administrations, Kennedy and Johnson, there was constant pressure to send more and more of the details to the President's desk. It probably applies to Nixon, too.

However, we have enormous communication capabilities already, and the very existence of the communication capability can act to handicap the achievement of the best decisions, in my opinion. It's a major question, and I don't think we will ever solve it to everybody's satisfaction.

Miss Kitchen: That's interesting, because the Bay of Pigs was certainly important.

Admiral Lee: I was not in the Atlantic Command for the Cuban missile crisis, but by collateral information I am pretty sure the same problems arose there that we had at the Bay of Pigs.

In short, too many decisions on details are made from Washington in ways that don't make good sense to people who are in the military professions and feel that there is a better way of doing it.

Miss Kitchen: Let us go on to the Commandant of National War College from 1964 until you retired.

Admiral Lee: It was a delightful three years. You were, or could be, cut in on practically everything that was going one nationally and internationally that you had the slightest interest in. You had the ability to guide, within limits, the curriculum in ways you considered to be the best for the national interest. You had the chance of - the obligation and responsibility really - being something of a father figure to a lot of intelligent, top-notch people, in their early forties, most of whom were probably going on to very important job

Miss Kitchen: In those three years you saw three hundred of the top officers of all of the services.

Admiral Lee: It used to be a hundred a year, when I was a student in '49, but it's now a hundred and forty - about four hundred and twenty in three years.

The Commandant is concerned with the structure of the lecture program - what lecturer should be approached to deliver a certain lecture - and this can become an interesting part of his duties. As an example, you want to have a top-notch speaker talk on the influence of the Communist Party in western Euro To get a top speaker in that field you have to go to all of the Communist party students all over the United States, most of them in the universities or special study centers, and you emer with say ten names. We had a council for selecting these peopl

You ask, "Is this the best man?" "Well, let's see --" approach. So you argue the advantages of having this person or that person, based on what people knew about them and their abilities as a speaker and many other things that crop up. Finally you say, "Smith from Dartmouth will be our first choice, and Jones from Harvard will be our second, and Brown from Stanford will be third on the list." It's taken an hour of argument to decide on these three names. Then you ask Smith and he can't come, and Brown can't come, and Jones can't come. And you're left with number four - whom you've forgotten all about and you didn't want anyway - he says he'll be glad to come.

This is the process you use in getting speakers on various topics that are more political than military - an awful lot of it is political. It isn't this way so much in the military phases of the lecture program, because there the choices are fairly clear cut. I would say roughly half of the speakers at the National War College are affiliated with universities. There are various cliques and schools of thoughts among the experts in each field in the universities - some opposed to each other, some highly regarded, and some highly regarded only in some circles. They are all top-drawer people, in and out of government.

Miss Kitchen: Would you sometimes get two men on different sides to present different opinions?

Admiral Lee; What you often wanted to do was to get two people to get up and debate their claims, but it's not easy to find two people to come and you'd have to pay them more -- the budget intrudes. But above all there's a prestige factor that gets into this. Brown and Smith won't get up and argue on the same platform like a couple of college debaters. They want to be the king pin and take all the questions and so forth They don't like to debate.

Miss Kitchen: And they don't want to let their opinion be put in question by having somebody talk on the other side probably.

Admiral Lee: That's right. I'm probably making too much of this right now. The question of the selection of the civilian professors to be hired to serve one or two year contracts on the staff of the National War College also is the subject of much debate. In sum, I feel that the Commandant of the National War College has many ways of influencing things which aren't apparent until after you've had the job, but they are important

Another example: We had required readings for the students each day, and after you've glanced through the required readings you see that such and such a person in your own staff is always recommending this kind of thing or that kind of thing which don't seem to be objective or present enough of the other side of the picture. We always try to present every side of the picture, and be as objective as we can.

All in all it's an extremely stimulating place. It's a great asset to the U. S. government. It has all kinds of hidden dividends for our country, I think - many of them unsuspected.

For instance, we do have a wide stable of people who want to come and talk to us - it's a prestigious thing to be able to come. Some of them come and get educated by spending the day with us, having questions fired at them by a hundred students who are themselves very well educated, experienced men in various fields. This shakes up some of the gentlemen from the Halls of Academe who haven't been bothered too much with non-academic viewpoints. I don't want to sound pompous, but I think we educated the denizens of the Halls of Academe a little bit.

I found the War College delightful. The social life there is pleasant, and I couldn't have asked for a better place to spend my last three years on active duty.

The Commandant's job is rotated among the Army, Navy, and Air Force. All the staff is similarly rotated. The College has never assumed any political or strategic school of thought. It hasn't espoused "isms" or been under the influence of any particular clique, so far as I know, and I don't think it ever will be.

Miss Kitchen: So you did retire from there in May '67, and you had served how many years in the Navy?

Admiral Lee: I entered the Naval Academy on June third, 1922 - forty-five years before I retired.

Miss Kitchen: What do you think your greatest contribution to your country or to the Navy has been?

Admiral Lee: It's hard for me to judge. I think my part in the creation and sustenance of our moral leadership program and the accent on leadership in the Naval Air Training Command probably had more influence than any other field I worked in. I was happy with what I was doing there. I think I contributed.

Miss Kitchen: Have you ever felt that you had any weakness?

Admiral Lee: Haven't we all? My problem is too many weaknesses, I guess.

I know I had a weakness in not saying "no" when I should have. I'm a person who is inclined to say "yes." There are times when you ought to be inclined so say 'yes' just for the sake of getting something done, but I'm talking about the weakness of knowing you ought to tell a guy off because he hasn't done a thing worth a damn and needs to shape up, and you dismiss him with, "All right, it's a nice afternoon, we'll let the matter go.

Looking back, I would say that I had probably not been good at what you might call force, or drive, in that sense.

Miss Kitchen: I have not been aware of that in your description of your duties. I have observed one thing in each duty that you had - you approached it as though it were a wonderful opportunity.

Admiral Lee: It always was.

One of my more interesting jobs was as a member of what was called the Pride Board, after Admiral Pride who was then a retired officer recalled for the prupose of being the senior member of a board of about seven or eight naval officers in the range of commander, captain, and admiral, some retired, and three civilians. This board was created because a Secretary of the Navy didn't get his protogé, who had been working as his aide, promoted to admiral. He concluded that there were cliques and other undesirable factors working in the admirals selection boards. He was mad because he couldn't force a selection board to select his man for admiral. So he appointed a board to inquire into how the Navy could obtain better admirals - what procedures were necessary to get a better quality of admiral in the Navy. That was the precept of the board.

We sat for about two and a half weeks, but this was Saturdays, Sundays, and up until eight or nine o'clock at night, because we wanted to get it done, and we were all busy at other jobs. We examined all the aspects we could dream up, and we came to the conclusion that the way to get better admirals in the Navy was to select better men at the bottom and treat them well all along the line, period. Not just when they were at the bottom - treat them well all the way up. If you did you were pretty sure to get good people out of the top. That seems a silly little distillation out of all the things we went through, but this is what we came up with, and I think we were right.

The three civilians appointed to the Pride Board were all prominent people. One was the personnel director of Standard Oil of New Jersey. He was not so much the personnel director as the supervisor of their specialized system for hunting for top leadership in Standard Oil. Another had the same job for J. C. Penny stores. And the third was a college professor, a specialist in psychological factors in selection of personnel.

The Board examined the fitness report and selection board systems at great length. All three of the civilian members were amazed by the fact that we had this selection system and used it the way we did. They said, "If we could only have this in our company, we'd be so far ahead of the game it would be marvelous." The head of the Standard Oil personnel selection system said, "If we had to operate under the same handicap that you do in some respects, Standard Oil would go broke in nothing flat, but if we had your selection system we would make more money."

I have been impressed through the years with the fact that people are people, and in personnel selection you are bound to make mistakes every once in a while. People change. A man will go along for years always well qualified to be promoted, and then you find he has gone through a change in his life or his attitudes, and he doesn't merit further promotion.

By and large, I think it would be very hard to devise a better system than the Navy's selection system. It has been copied by the Army and Air Force. We haven't always been allowed to make it work the way it should, and it hasn't done too good at times, but for some historian who wants to get a good look at the problems of the Navy in the choice of leaders in the fifties and sixties, a copy of the Pride Board report in the files of the Navy would be a good place to dig.

Miss Kitchen: Did the Secretary of the Navy accept the report? He couldn't very well do anything else. Did he like it?

Admiral Lee: He received it; I don't think he liked it.

When I said he couldn't change it, this is a hundred percent true. Anything can be turned down by the man at the top of any organization if he - the President - wants to do it. The U. S. President is the top man in the Navy. He can break the law and probably the law makers won't get after him for it if it is a comparatively minor matter, and one which he particularly wants. The same can be true of the Secretary of the Navy. The selection boards are all governed by law, but they can be circumvented. A Secretary can prevent an officer from being promoted to admiral, but he can't tell a selection board not to nominate him and to select Joe Blow instead. He can refuse to approve any man on the list for promotion.

They tried this in the case of Admiral Burke. Mr. Truman said he wouldn't have Captain Burke as an admiral; the selection board would have to find somebody else. The selection board just said, "We won't do it." But the person Truman wanted was subsequently selected by writing into the specifications of a subsequent selection board detailed specifications which could only apply to that one man. That's the one way they they can do it, and that's the way it has been done – it's wrong.

I believe that the Navy personnel system from almost every point of view is a very fine one. Although we don't bat a hundred, we do so much better than most other organizations that I think we have something to be proud of.

Miss Kitchen: I'm sure the Navy has much occasion to be proud of you in your service. You did get the second DSM for your last job.

Admiral Lee: DSMs are mostly just pats on the back as you walk off stage.

INDEX

to interviews with

Fitzhugh Lee

Vice Admiral, U. S. Navy (Retired)

AKAGI - CV: at Battle of Midway, 35

American Missionaries In China, comments on, 42

ANCON, 175

Anderson, Jack, 187

ANTIETAM (USS), flagship, 239; visit to Canada, 239

APPALACHIAN, command ship, 201

ARDENT, HMS, 39

Aruba, 56; German SS attack on tankers and tanks at Aruba, 57-58

Asiatic Fleet, duty with, 31; tours in Japan to inspect aviation installations, 31-33; aviation units with fleet, 35-37

AUGUSTA, USS, CA, 37-38; enroute to ship, 38-40; trip to Chungking, 41-42; 78-79; return home via Japanese freighter, 44-45

Australia, visit for Coral Sea Memorial Week, 260-264

Aviation Representative, ONI, 30

Baldwin, Hanson, 194

Baltimore, USS, cruiser, 99

Barksdale Field, La., 285

Bay of Pigs Operation, 291-299; discovery of existing plans for invasion, 293; White House changes landing location, 294; event unfolds, 295-296; failure to rescue group calling for help, 296; discussion of role of President in military command, 297-299; role of increased communication facilities, 298-299

Belgian Congo, 289-290; problems in policing, 290

BENNINGTON, USS, CV, 275, 260-262

Betty - name for Japanese plane; names given by ONI for convenience, 97-98

Bikini, 200, 206

Bingham, Barry, 148

Bogan, VADM Gerald F., 46-47, 214; on morale in naval forces, 218

Bonin Islands, casemate constructed for art treasures, 245-246

Bradley, Gen. Omar - testifies in B-36 controversy, famous 'fancy dans' remakr, 219

Brent School, Philippines, 2-3

Bullen Bay, Aruba, 56

Bunker Hill, CV (USS), 111

Burke, Admiral Arleigh, 243, 293; role in Bay of Pigs operation, 295; President Truman withholds selection to flag rank, 308

Camp McGrath, 4

CarDiv Five, 256 ff

The Case Against the Admirals, a book, 185-186

CHEFOO, China, 42

Chiang Kai-shek, 247

Chief of Information: duty with Adm. Nimitz, 145; correspondents on Guam, 147-149; VIPs, 150; reaction to atomic bomb, 154; accreditation of correspondents to Nimitz and Gen. LeMay, 156; attempts of certain press members to create problems, 157; Lee's duty as Chief Censor of Pac Ocean Area, 158-159; problem with policy of navy as 'silent service,' 161-162; contrasted with policy of Air Force, 163-164; Okinawa and the press, 168-169; plans for invasion of Japan and the press, 169; surrender ceremony, 169-170; dealing with Russian correspondents, 171-174; press and first visits to Tokyo, 175-176

CIA (Central Intelligence Agency), 292-293

CincLant Command: Lee serves as Deputy to Admiral Dennison, 287; discussion of various problems of command, 287 ff.

CincSouth - creation of command, 288; headquarters in Panama, 288

Clark, RADM John E., 294

Clark, Admiral J. (Jocko) J., 82

Coblenz, Germany, 4

Colombia Airline, 51-52

ComAirPac, 73-75

Combat Fatigue, problems concerning, 108-109

ComCarDiv 14, command of A/S Carrier group, 239

ComFltAir, Japan, 240 ff.

Considine, Robert (Bob), 203

Cook, RADM A. B., 22, 28

Coral Sea Memorial Week in Australia, 260-264

Coronet, code name for proposed Japanese invasion, 150

Corrigan, Dr. Frank, U. S. Ambassador to Venezuela, 62

Costa Rica, 62

CPO Leadership School, at Pensacola, 285-286; standards, 286

Cuba, 292, area of CincLant responsibility

Cuban Missile Crisis, 299

Cubi Point, 241

Dairen, 43-44

Dennison, Adm. Robert Lee, 198, 274, 277-279, 285, 287, 292, 295

Derevyanko, General Kuzma, 172

Dillon, The Hon. Douglas, 107

Diller, General: Public Information office for General MacArthur, 16

D'Olier, Franklin, Chairman, U. S. Strategic Bombing Survey, Germany and Japan, 252-253, 255

Dollar Line, 79

Douhet Theory, 20-21; 213; 251

DSM (Distinguished Service Medal), comments on, 284

Duerfeldt, RADM Clifford H., 18

Duncan, Admiral Donald, 82

Educational System in the U. S., comments on, 266-274; additional comments, college level, 275-276

Eisenhower, President Dwight D., 269

Enola Gay, plane that dropped atomic bomb on Japan, 153

ENTERPRISE, CV, 48-49

ESSEX, USS, CV, 61, 81-82; conflagration station episode, 84; 85, 87; comments on ESSEX class CVs, 88, 90-91; outline of duties on ESSEX, 96-97; 98; citation, 100; remarks about morale aboard, 100-101; whiskey problem solved, 102; proxy marriage while on board, 103-106, 128

Fala, ship rescue helicopter on carrier FDR, 228-229

Felt, Admiral Charles Donald, 18

Fighter Squadron 5, 18, later Squadron 6, 48, 76

Fighting Lady, 86, see also entries for ESSEX and YORKTOWN, carriers

Fitch, Admiral Aubrey W., 73

Fitzhugh Committee, 220-221

Forrestal, The Hon. James, 184; unification struggle, 190-191; Secretary of Defense, 191; Sullivan-Symington feud, 194-195, 197, his final days, 207-208

FRANKLIN D. ROOSEVELT, USS, CV: Lee's tour of duty in command, 222-

229; ship's newspaper, 225-227; morale and leadership, 228

Freedom of the Press, 158-160, 166-167, 188; The Chicago Tribune and the story on breaking of the Japanese code, 189-190; failure to punish, 190, 202; Bikini and irresponsibility, 203-204

Fulbright Memorandum, 272, 283

Gardner, ADM M. B., 224

Genda, Gen. Minoru, 242-243

Goldthwaite, VADM Robert, 272, 283, 285

Griffin, ADM Charles D., proxy wife on ESSEX, 104

Gros, Robert R., 196-197

Guadalcanal, battle, 90-91

Guam, Command Headquarters, 146-147, 154, 156

Gulf of Paria, 59

Gygax, RADM Felix Xerxes, 79

Halsey, ADM Wm., 16-17, 47, 49, 85, 127, 177-178; reaction to Japan, 178-179

Harding President Warren G., 6

Hedding, VADM Truman J., 113

Hells Angels, movie, 18-19

Heron, Seaplane Tender, 36

Hickham Field, 74

Hiroshima, 152, 247-248; museum of the atom bomb blast, 248-249

Honshu, 258

Hoover, President Herbert, 23-24

Hopkins, Harry, 26

HORNET, USS, CV, 73

Howe, Col. Louis, 26

Huie, William Bradford, author, 186

Ignatius, The Hon. Paul, 129

Iwo Jima Press Release, 165-166

Japan, 241 ff., distinctive culture, 244; attitude towards art treasures, 245-246; customs, 247-248; WWII underground installations 249-252

Japanese Naval Aviation, 247

Jennings, VADM Ralph E., 49

Johnson, Secretary Louis, 198

Johnson, Stanley, Chicago Tribune reporter, 189-190

Joint Task Force Four, creation of, 289; use of, 290

Kaiser Class, Jeep Carriers, comments on construction, 115-116, 135

Kamikaze, 130, 132; description of a kamikaze pilot and his dress, 141-142, 144

KEARSARGE (USS), 257

Kennedy, President John F., 221

King, Fleet Admiral Ernest J., 76-77, called to testify in B-36 controversy, 218

Kinshasa (ex-Leopoldville), 290

Kissner, Gen. August, Public Information Office for Gen. LeMay, 161

Korean War, 210

Kurita, Admiral, Japanese admiral in battle of Leyte Gulf, 119-121, 124

Lake Maracaibo, 56

Lee, VADM Fitzhugh: geneology, 1-2; early history, 2-6; publishes article as j.g. that attracts attention, 22; marriage by proxy, 103-106; marriage in San Francisco, 144-145; Rear Admiral,

259-260; Vice Admiral, 285

LeMay, Gen. Curtis, 156; commander of 20th Air Force Strategic Air Command, 156; 161

LEXINGTON, USS, commissioning, 11; duty on, 12-13; 76-77; the new Lex, 93; based at Pensacola for training, 282

Leyte, 118-119, 140

Lingayen Gulf, 118, 127, 129, 137

Luce, Henry, 150

MacArthur, General Douglas, 86; Cinc SoWesPac, 156-7; 160-161; 170

Manhattan Project, 152-154

Manila, 118, 176

Manila Bay (USS), jeep carrier, 114, 117, 122, 127-128; kamikaze attack, 133-138, 139, 140, 142-143

Manus Island, 117, 129

Maracay, 66

Marcus Island operation, 87, 89

Martin, VADM William I., rescue at Truk, 99

Matthews, The Hon. Francis P., Secretary of the Navy, 215=217

McMorris, VADM C. H., 152, 165

Memphis, Tenn.: location of N. A. Tech Training Command, 265

Midway, Battle of, 73

Military-Industrial Complex, 195-196

Miller, RADM H. B. (Min), 145-146, 183

Mindoro, 129

MISSOURI, USS, BB, 85-86, 88

Mitchell, General Billy, 20

Mitscher, Admiral Marc Andrew, 111; decision to light decks for landing, 113

Monterey, Calif., 199

Mt. Hood, ammunition ship, 117

Moorer, Admiral Thomas, 252

Musashi, Japanese battleship, 121-123

Mydans, Carl and Sheffey, 151-152

Nagasaki, 152

Nagasawa, Admiral, Japanese Chief of Naval Operations, 247

NAS (Naval Air Station) Atsugi, 240; WWII installations, 249

Naval Air Station, Coco Solo, 63, 65

NAS (Naval Air Station), Norfolk: Lee's command of, 229-238; civil service problems, 230; Drew Pearson story, 230-231; race problems, 232-234; noise problems, 234-235; general court martial for two pilots, 236-237; case before Civil Service Commission, 237-238

NAS (Naval Air Station), Pensacola, 13-14, 22, return from Asiatic Fleet, 44; flight instructor, 46, 285-286

NAS (Naval Air Station), Willow Grove, 235-236

National Security Act of 1947, 190

National War College, 208-210, speakers, 209; value of associations, 239-240; Lee as Commandant, 297, 300; concerns as Commandant, 300-301; selection of speakers, 300-303

NATO, 287

NATO Navies: comments on, 224-225

Naval Air Technical Training Command, 264; purpose of command, 265, 266; comments on education in U. S. and its bearing on training in this command, 266-268; system of teaching as employed in command, 269-271; speed up of program for teaching mathematics, 269; effort to tell armed services and public of success in teaching program, 272; program Lee utilized as Chief of Naval Air Training, 274

Naval Air Training: Lee serves as Chief, 274; recruitment problems, 275-276; Naval Reserve Training Command, 274, 276-277; newsletter to build morale and leadership, 277; how N. A. training differs from rest of navy, 280-281; scope of job, 282; training flight surgeons, 282-283; courses in 'communism vs Americanism,' 284; estimate of achievements in this command, 304

Naval aviation: flight training, 13-14; screening test, 14; catapult training, 14-15; training in ship gunfire spotting, 15; details of Pensacola training, 16; early fleet maneuvers to demonstrate carrier power, 19; article on carrier design, 22

Navy Postgraduate School, new site, 199

Newport News Shipbuilding Co., 82-83; attitude of workers in wartime, 83

Newsletters, N. A. Technical Training Command, 277; Lant Leader, 277; CNATRA Dope, 277; comments, 278-280

Nimitz, Fleet Admiral Chester W., 37, 73-75, 77-79, 85, 145-146; in Guam, 151-152, 153-154; staff conferences on Guam, 154-156; 157; Nimitz and MacArthur, 160; Nimitz and Press Conferences, 165, 173; reflections on Nimitz, 179-180-181-182; protocol for seating, 180; called to testify in B-36 controversy, 218

Nitze, The Hon. Paul, Secretary of the Navy, 252

Nomura, Admiral, Japanese Ambassador to Washington, 243

Ofstie, VADM Ralph, 32, 91, 95, 252; conflict with air force over

- 9 -

appendix to Strategic Bombing Report, 254

Ogilby, Remson B., educator, 2-3

Okinawa: picture of invasion, 168; dealing with the reporters during invasion, 168

OKLAHOMA, BB, 11-12, 14

Olathe, Kansas, 266

OMMANEY BAY, jeep carrier (USS), 130-131

Operation Crossroads, 200; Lee in charge of Public relations for event, 200-201; press accommodations, 201; priority with dispatches, 202-203; physical comfort and bearing on quality of news stories, 205, 206

Oppama, Japan, 34; naval research center, 34; incident of the Martin Flying Boat, 34

Pallbearer, Duties of honorary, 22

Panama, civil strife, 288-289

PANAY, gunboat, 41

Parsons, RADM W. S., 153

Pearl Harbor, 73, 81, 107

Pearl Harbor day in Panama, 62-63; blackout, 64-66

Pearson, Drew, 187; attitude towards Secretary Forrestal, 208; incident at NAS, Norfolk, 230-232; 2nd story about the NAS, Norfolk, 235

Pecos, Seaplane Tender, 36

Philippine Sea, battle of, 111-114; overall plan for invasion, 118; details of battle, 120-127

Phoebus, Captain, flight surgeon, 282

Port Arthur, 43; description of Naval Base, 44

PRAVDA, 171, 173

Pride, Admiral A. M., 222, 224

Pride Board, purpose of its creation, 305; work of Board, 305-306; business representatives on board, 306

PTA, 268-269

Public Relations Office, Navy Department: two specific concerns, 183-184; unification issue, 183-185; reserve recruiting program, 184-185

Rabaul, 90, 92

Radar, use at Guadalcanal, 91; at Tarawa, 93

Radford, Admiral Arthur, CincPacFlt, 210; Lee serves as Assistant Chief of Staff, 210; role of CincPacFlt in Korean War, 210; role of B-36 controversy, 213-217, 220-221

Rainbow 5, 68

Recruiting Program, Reserves, 184-185

RED RIPPERS (See Fighter Squadron 5)

Revere Silver, gift to LEXINGTON (USS), 12

Revolt of the Admirals, 212-217; report of the hearings before the Committee of the House of Representatives, 219-220

Rivero, Adm. Horacio, Jr., 295

Robbins, RADM Thomas H., Jr., 190

Roosevelt, Mrs. F. D. 27

Roosevelt, President F. D., 23, 25-26; 50

Russell, Adm. J. S., 88-89, 252

Sgahalien, 241

San Bernardino Strait, 118-119

San Diego, Calif., 14

Sangley Pt., 241

Sasaki, Ahiro, Japanese aviator, 35

Sasebo: WW II oil storage tanks, 250

Service rivalry: early controversy, 19-20

Sevres, France, 5

Shanghai, China, 78

Sherman, Admiral Forrest, 146, 152, 165

Spruance, Admiral Raymond, 75, 113

Stassen, Harold, 85-86

Strategic Bombing Survey, War in the Pacific: 251-256; President Truman asks for certain recommendations in report, 255-256

Strike Command: creation of, 287-288

Stroop, VADM Paul D., 18'

Stump, Admiral Felix, 125, 138, 260, reaction to Coral Sea Memorail Week prank, 263-264

Sullivan, The Hon. John, Secretary of the Navy, 191-192, 194-195, resignation, 198-199

Sulu Sea, 130

Surigao Strait, 118-119, 127, 140

Symington, Senator Stuart, 192-193; conflict with Secretary Sullivan, 193-195, 221

Tachikawa Air Field, 244

Tarawa, 92

Taylor, RADM Ford N., 30

Thompson, J. Walter, agency, 184-185

TICONDEROGA (USS), CV, 257

Tinian, 154

Togo, Admiral, 247

Tokyo, 176; condition of city upon entry of Americans, 177

Tokyo Rose, 175-177

Tomlinson, Capt. Daniel W. (Tommy), 49

Trinidad, 59-60

Truk, 98

Truman, President Harry S., 196-199; policy on Israel, 207; effect on Secretary Forrestal, 207; asks for specific recommendations from Strategic Bombing Survey, 255; refuses selection of Arleigh Burke, 308

Tsingtao, China, 42

Tyloer, Harriet Davis, 2nd wife of Admiral Lee, 46

Unification controversy, 183-185, 190-191, 194-195, navy vs air force, 193-194; in Korean War, 211-212; 'revolt of the Admirals,' 212-217; report of hearings before House Committee, 219-220; role of Admiral Radford in B-36 controversy, 213-217, 220-221

United States (USS), CV, 198, 213

U. S. Air Force, controversy over the Strategic Bombing Report in the Pacific, 252 ff.

U. S. Naval Academy: details of Lee appointment, 6; recollections of Academy days, 7-9; value of class associations, 8-9; summer program in aviation, 10

Venezuela: naval attache to Caracas, 50; nazi propaganda and sub-rosa commission in FBI, 51; use of Jewish refugees, 52; use of Basques, 53; protective measures for Panama Canal, 54-55; naval control and shipping officer, north coast of South

America, 58-61, 62; return from trip from Central America and situation in Embassy, 66, 68; at war, 69; exploration of Oronoco and Amazon river systems, 70-72

Vinson, The Hon. Carl, member of Congress, 217

Wagner, VADM Frank Dechant, 106-108

Wainwright, Gen. Jonathan Mayhew, 86

War Plans Division, Navy Department: two year tour of duty, 22, 28; Orange and Rainbow plans, 29; focus on trust territories, 29

WASP, USS, carrier, 107-108

Whangpoo River, China, 78-79

White House, participation in Bay of Pigs operation, 295, 297

White House aide, duties of, 22-23; use of memory course, 24, 25-28

Willoughby, Gen. Charles A., 172-173

YAMATO, Japanese battleship, 121

Yangtze River trip, 41

Yokosuka Naval Station, 178

YORKTOWN, USS, CV, 49, 82, 85, 87, 90

www.ingramcontent.com/pod-product-compliance
Lightning Source LLC
Chambersburg PA
CBHW080617170426
43209CB00007B/1455